Camara Laye

Twayne's World Authors Series
French Literature

David O'Connell, Editor
University of Illinois

TWAS 695

CAMARA LAYE
(1928–1980)
Photograph courtesy of
Plon Publishers, Paris

Camara Laye

By Sonia Lee
Trinity College

Twayne Publishers • Boston

Camara Laye

Sonia Lee

Copyright © 1984 by G. K. Hall & Company
All Rights Reserved
Published by Twayne Publishers
A Division of G. K. Hall & Company
70 Lincoln Street
Boston, Massachusetts 02111

Book Production by Marne B. Sultz

Book Design by Barbara Anderson

Printed on permanent/durable acid-free
paper and bound in the United States of America.

Library of Congress Cataloging in Publication Data.

Lee, Sonia.
  Camara Laye.

  (Twayne's world authors series ; TWAS 695)
  Bibliography: p. 121
    Includes index.
    1. Camara, Laye—Criticism and interpretation.
I. Title. II. Series.
PQ3989.C27Z75   1984   843   83-12780
ISBN 0-8057-6542-5

Contents

About the Author

Sonia Lee is Associate Professor of French at Trinity College in Hartford, Connecticut. She completed the Ph.D. at the University of Massachusetts, Amherst, in 1974.

Her work has appeared, among other places, in the *Yale French Review, Critique,* the *French Review* and *Arts & Lettres,* the literary magazine of *Soleil,* Dakar, Senegal.

Preface

The contemporary Western African novel, whether in French or in English, is for the most part sociological in content and satirizes the society it depicts. This is not true, however, of Camara Laye's work, which is highly poetic in tone and spiritual in content; indeed, his entire output can be characterized by the English title of his third book, *A Dream of Africa*. For this reason, Camara Laye[1] has been labeled a traditionalist, not necessarily a compliment in postindependence Africa, and he has until recently been much criticized by certain elements of the African intelligentsia. The subject of Laye's controversial position in African literature will be examined in chapter 2, along with his significance as a writer.

Although Camara Laye writes in prose, his vision is that of the poet and this study focuses primarily on his symbols and imagery, in an attempt to show that his work can be seen as a kaleidoscopic vision of Africa, a series of metaphoric variations on the same theme, with a definite reverence toward the past, its values, its history, and its myths, along with an unshakable faith in the future.

This essay is divided into three parts. The first analyzes as a single entity both *L'Enfant noir* and *Dramouss,* his first and third books, since they constitute an autobiographical sequel and are both dominated by the same protagonists. They are, however, quite different in intent. *L'Enfant noir* is the cornerstone of Laye's fiction, for it contains the key to his metaphorical language and poetic imagination, derived mostly from his parents' mythical beliefs and values, whereas *Dramouss* is the most evident example of metaphorical transference. The second part is devoted to *Le Regard du roi,* considered to be Camara Laye's masterpiece. With this novel we penetrate into the author's psyche, an imaginary world animated with the spirits and visions of his ancestors, a mysterious universe full of mute symbols and cryptic messages in which the image of Africa is spiritualized into an oneiric and intangible Africa of the mind, explored through the quest and moral anguish of the main character, a white man lost in Africa and seeking his salvation. Third, in *Le Maître de la parole,* Laye's last work, the author takes on the role of the medieval cleric of the European tradition, and transcribes the words of the ancient bard. The book is a version of the epic poem of the Malinké people,[2] the story of the great hero *Soundiata,* which has been sung since the thirteenth century, and it is only fitting that Camara Laye's final vision of Africa should be a glorious one, in perfect keeping with the spirit of his first book. *L'Enfant noir* was written in order to remember his own childhood and his homeland, and *Le Maître de la parole* to enable Africa to remember her past.

As many African critics point out,[3] it is imperative to analyze the work of an African writer primarily in its cultural context and as the reflection of a specific civilization. Consequently, the documentation and justification of this analysis frequently rely on Malinké's myths, concepts, and social structure. Culturally, however, Camara Laye was also a Frenchman and very much at ease with that fact. He borrowed from Western civilization what suited him best. His stylistic master was Flaubert, and he found in Kafka the dreamlike structure which he considered totally in harmony with his African temperament. Therefore, a critical approach of a somewhat protean nature is called for. Concerning his work, no single method of criticism can be followed systematically, but rather the critic must borrow from many in order to encompass better the subject.

This essay does not aim to be an exhaustive study of Camara Laye's work, but rather an analysis of the artist's poetic vision of his culture and of the world. His two short stories will not be analyzed as such, but mentioned for reference as the need arises. It should be added that the author has left an unpublished manuscript which will most likely not be published for some years, because of the political difficulties it could possibly cause his family.

To the best of my knowledge, there is only one full-length study devoted to Camara Laye, namely Adèle King's *The Writings of Camara Laye* (London: Heineman, 1980). I am most grateful to Miss King for letting me read her excellent study while it was still in manuscript. There are, however, numerous articles devoted to Laye's work and the most important ones are listed in the Bibliography.

All English translations in this essay are my own, except where otherwise indicated.

I wish to thank Reine Carducci for being so kind and so helpful, le Commandant Thierno, Professor Yves Person, Jacqueline Sorel of Radio France, and Hélène Bourgeois of Librairie Plon who allowed me to consult the author's files. I should like to thank Camara Laye's children Aichat Marie Chantal (Fifi) and Alassane for sharing the memory of their father with me, and Madame Ramatoulaye Camara Kanté for receiving me into her home. I am most grateful to my colleague Ken Lloyd-Jones, who kindly consented to proofread the initial draft of the manuscript and whose helpful advice was deeply appreciated.

Sonia Lee

Trinity College

Chronology

1928   Camara Laye born in Kouroussa, Upper Guinea.

1942   Goes to Conakry, the capital of Guinea, to continue his studies.

1947   He leaves for France with a scholarship to study engineering in Paris. To earn a living he works at night in les Halles, Paris's general food market.

1953   Publishes *L'Enfant noir* (Plon). Marries his Guinean sweetheart, Marie Lorofi, in Paris.

1954   In February he receives the Prix Charles Veillon for *L'Enfant noir*. In November, publishes *Le Regard du roi* (Plon). Goes back to Guinea for a short trip.

1956   Returns to Africa with his wife. First to Dahomey (now Bénin), then to Ghana.

1963   Participates in the Conference on African Literature, held at the University of Dakar, Senegal, and a month later at Fourah Bay College in Freetown, Sierra Leone.

1963–1965   Is associate director of the National Institute of Research and Documentation.

1965   Leaves Guinea for political reasons with his family for Dakar.

1966   Publishes *Dramouss* (Plon).

1970   His wife, Marie, goes back to Guinea and is imprisoned for seven years.

1975   Becomes ill and is hospitalized in Dakar. Mrs. Carducci launches an appeal to raise funds to pay for medical expenses.

1977   Marie is released from prison.

1978   *Le Maître de la parole* (Plon), his last published work.

1980   Dies in Dakar of hypertensive nephritis.

Chapter One
Paradise Lost

Camara Laye, the oldest son of a rather large family, was born in Kouroussa, Upper Guinea, on 1 January 1928. Guinea, a former French colony, is a small West African country and its upper region is characterized by tall grass savannahs through which the river Niger flows; its population is predominantly Malinké. Laye, as a Malinké, belongs to one of the most important ethnic groups that form the Manding culture. The Malinké are distinguished by a glorious history and it is believed that they have occupied Guinean territory since the thirteenth century, the time of Soundiata, founder of the Empire of Mali. As a Camara, our author belongs to one of the oldest Malinké clans, and his name, along with the Keita, Traoré, and Kourouma, is still prominent in the region. Due to their strong social structure, the Malinké have maintained their culture, and often imposed it on other ethnic groups; at present, their language is spreading and becoming the lingua franca of the Western Sudan.[1]

Like most Malinké, Laye was a Moslem and went to Koranic school before going to the French elementary school in his hometown. His father, Camara Komady, a native of Kouroussa, was both a blacksmith and a goldsmith; his mother, Dâman Sadan, daughter of a blacksmith, was born in Tindican, a small village near Kouroussa. This large village on the river Niger, 700 kilometers from the coast, has been the cradle of Laye's family for generations, and it was between his father's and mother's birthplaces that the author spent his childhood, which he so aptly described in *L'Enfant noir*. Despite the colonial regime and the French school (the teachers were African), the white man's presence was hardly felt in Kouroussa and Laye reports that when he was a child, "there were only two French people in the town, a government official and his wife, whose life style was not like ours, they did not live like the Malinké."[2] Thus the author spent the important formative years of his life in a very traditional Malinké setting, watching his father smelting gold and working metal, and living in his mother's loving and dignified presence. As a child, he went through the rituals of Kondén Diara, the ceremony of the lions, a

1

frightening albeit safe ordeal that young boys must endure, to learn
how to conquer their fear. Laye recalled the event in *L'Enfant noir*.
He explained that Kondén Diara was a test reserved for uncircum-
cised boys. It usually occurred just before the beginning of Ramadan,
which is the Islamic Lent. The boys were taken by their elders into
the forest, to spend the night. After what seemed a long walk, they
arrived in a clearing and sat around a reassuring fire, when all of a
sudden, they heard the frightening roaring of lions which appeared to
be all around them. As they listened to the terrifying noise, they
were told to keep their heads down and to remain calm. Self-control
was clearly the issue. Although the ordeal was quite real and truly
terrorizing to the young boys, they were never in any danger, the
lions being pure adult mystification.

Later on Laye participated in the elaborate ceremonial of circumcision as it has been lived by young Malinké boys since time immemorial. There was no drama in Laye's childhood; it was a happy time
and understandably so, for the child was not aware of the latent
threat posed by the white man's presence to his culture and way of
life. This ignorance of the foreign world is made clear at the beginning of *L'Enfant noir*, when the narrator points out that his father's
compound was on the edge of the railroad tracks and that the sun-
heated rails attracted snakes which he was forbidden to play with.
The railroad, a symbol of the white man's power, brings out nothing
but the usual childish curiosity in the protagonist, and no further
comments from the author than that it attracted snakes. The bound-
aries of the boy's world were very limiting, and the infrequent trains
were, before his school years, most likely the only contact he had
with the nontraditional African world. Family life was happy and
peaceful, and it can be said that a happy childhood is the source of
Camara Laye's inspiration and idealism. The dramas and sorrows that
were to mark his life in later years, and there were many, did not
succeed in obliterating the happy memories of his earlier years, but
rather sustained his natural optimism. For Laye, Africa remained forever the Africa of his youth, and he was always to look upon her with
the eyes of the heart.

Going to French school in Kouroussa was not dramatic, it was
merely different. It set him apart from those who did not go, like his
country cousins on his mother's side, who, being destined to work
the land, did not need the white man's knowledge. It was only after
obtaining his *certificat d'Etudes* that the drama of separation began. In

order to continue his studies, he had to go to Conakry, the capital of Guinea, many miles from home. There, he went to the Collège Poiret, a vocational school opened in the 1930s. While in Conakry, he met his future wife, Marie Lorofi, whose father was a doctor. He did well in school and was awarded first place in the examinations for the *certificat d'Aptitude professionnelle de mécanicien;* this won him a scholarship to continue his studies in Paris, and he left for France in 1947. It was his first taste of exile, and leaving home, family, friends, and sweetheart was a traumatic experience which he relates vividly in the last chapter of *L'Enfant noir.* In France, he began his studies in the automobile school of Argenteuil, a suburb of Paris, and became a fully certified auto mechanic. Laye wanted to further his education but his scholarship was not renewed. He was told that Guinea did not need an engineer but an automobile specialist, so he did odd jobs to support himself. He worked at night in Les Halles, which was then Paris's general food market, as well as at the Simca auto plant, where he was a skilled worker for eight months. Meanwhile, he studied to pass his *baccalauréat,* took night classes "aux Arts et Métiers" (one of France's main technical institutions) and went to L'Ecole d'Ampère, from which he received a *Brevet d'enseignement industriel.* In 1953, the year that saw the publication of *L'Enfant noir,* he wrote, "I am presently studying at the Ecole technique d'aéronautique et de construction automobile to obtain un diplôme d'ingénieur calculateur"[3] (a diploma in industrial engineering).

Life in Paris

What was Paris like in the early 1950s for a young African? It was cold and lonely, but also exciting and enriching. Laye described his student life on many occasions, but he put it all together in the second chapter of *Dramouss,* entitled "Une nuit blanche." He understood many things about Africa from being in Paris, and one of them was African art, which he learned to appreciate in the Musée de l'homme. Distance sharpened his understanding of the motherland at the same time that it deepened his feelings for it and emphasized the importance of his own culture. His experiences in Paris were not much different from those of many of his contemporaries, and the adventures of a young African in Paris are the theme of many novels of the period. As early as 1937, Ousmane Socé, in *Les Mirages de Paris,* had described the difficult life of a young Senegalese in the French capital.

A few years after *L'Enfant noir,* Bernard Dadié published *Un nègre à Paris* (1959), and a year later, Aké Loba told the pathetic story of *Kocoumbo, l'étudiant noir. L'Aventure ambiguë* (1961) of Ch. H. Kane also has a chapter dedicated to Samba Diallo's student life in Paris. All these young African intellectuals, whom the critic Robert Pageard labels the generation of 1928, Laye's generation, have, regardless of their different backgrounds, shared many experiences: French schools, exile, and an often difficult homecoming. They were young at an exciting time, when colonial power was crumbling and African independence was in the making. They shared a crucial moment of twentieth-century African history, when all hopes were allowed and all dreams possible. Most African writers of the 1928 generation not only published abundantly in the 1950s and 1960s, but were also actively involved in the political changes that were occurring in their respective countries, hoping to play an important role after independence. This promising generation followed in the footsteps of the "Négritude generation," those who, in a sense, made everything possible or at least easier.

Négritude has been much discussed, much praised, and much maligned.[4] It germinated in the French West Indies but came into flower in Paris in the 1930s with *La Revue du Monde noir,* created by two Haitians, Dr. Sajons and Miss Nordal. This review propagated the ideas of the American Negro Renaissance, which considerably influenced the French-speaking elite. It was shortlived, and died out after six issues. However, the seed of revolt and self-consciousness had been sown, and in 1932, a group of West Indians published the inflammatory *Légitime Défense,* which was censured immediately. This new review denounced among other things the alienation of the Antilles bourgeoisie, its fatal imitation of French culture, and its betrayal of its own race and cultural heritage. It went farther than straight criticism, as it pledged to change the situation by fighting for the black race on all fronts. Revolutionary ideas, be they political, social, or artistic, were not foreign to the post–World War I Parisian intelligentsia. It suffices to remember that the Surrealist movement had already had an impact on the artistic world, and on poetry in particular; that in 1925 Gide, with *Les Faux-Monneyeurs,* had proposed to transform the novel as Proust had already succeeded in doing a few years earlier. *L'Art nègre* had been discovered at the beginning of the century and had influenced Cubism; Africa entered the mainstream of Modern Art before the "Exposition des Arts Décoratifs" of

1925, and "L'Exposition coloniale" of 1931 had revealed it to the general public. In 1921, Blaise Cendrars had published his *Anthologie nègre,* glorifying the diversity of African languages and the cultures that they expressed. Paris was then the intellectual Mecca of the Western world and the perfect terrain for new ideas. In 1934, a small review, *L'Etudiant noir,* appeared, founded by three African students who were all to become very famous: Léopold Sédar Senghor from Senegal, Aimé Césaire from Martinique, and Léon Damas from French Guyana. It was they who elaborated the notion of Négritude; the word itself was coined by Césaire in 1939, in *Cahier d'un retour au pays natal,* but it was Senghor who became and remained its most eloquent theoretician: "La négritude est le patrimoine culturel, les valeurs et surtout l'esprit de la civilisation négro-africaine."[5] The war interrupted the publication of *L'Etudiant noir,* but in 1947 there appeared, simultaneously in Paris and in Dakar, the review *Présence Africaine,* founded by Alioune Diop and a group of young writers. This review was sponsored by such personalities as Gide, Sartre, Mounier, Leiris, Senghor, Césaire, Richard Wright, and others. With *Présence Africaine* the black world had a strong voice, a forum from which to speak and to be heard by the world.[6]

Despite the loneliness of exile, the years that Laye spent in Paris, between 1947 and 1956, were fruitful and stimulating. Independence was in the making and literary production was prodigious. The Triumvirate of Négritude was already well known for its literary output, and by the 1950s Césaire had published several collections of poems, as had also Senghor and Damas. Senghor's *Anthologie de la nouvelle poésie nègre et malgache de langue française* (1948) brought attention to a wide array of promising young poets, and Négritude poetry constitutes without a doubt the finest corpus of poetry of modern Africa. The anthology presented poets of the new generation, Laye's generation, which has been to this day, in poetry and in prose, the most prolific in African letters, and counts such names as Ch. H. Kane, Olympe Bhely-Quenum, Ferdinand Oyono, Tchicaya U'Tamsi, Mongo Beti (a few years younger, but whose work was published between 1954 and 1958). It can therefore hardly be said that Laye wrote in an intellectual desert, but his *L'Enfant noir,* an autobiographical novel, can nevertheless be considered as a pioneer work because of its artistic value and the genre used. Up to that date, the best black francophone literary production had been in poetry. In prose, only a few works were artistically important: *Batouala* of René

Maran (prix Goncourt 1921); *Doguicimi* of Paul Hazoumé (1935); and the remarkable *Contes d'Amadou Koumba* of Birago Diop (1947). Many other works were published, but their literary merit is not up to their sociological importance. *L'Enfant noir* was very well received and also highly controversial and it brought fame to its author. When he went home for a short visit in 1954, his trip turned into a triumph. His success at home and in France was sustained by the publication of *Le Regard du roi* in 1954, considered by many critics as a masterpiece, which made of its author a major writer in African letters.

The main controversy surrounding his work came from his fellow African writers because his books were not politically committed at a time when it seemed impossible not to be. Yet he was a political man in the sense that he kept abreast of the political situation in France and at home, and in his beautiful portrayal of African life and culture. He was, however, too conservative for his time. While in Paris, he was in favor of the French Union, that is, the particular rapport between France and its colonies, and later, for the French Community. He did favor independence, but wanted to maintain strong cultural, social, and economic ties with France. He was an idealist; Adèle King tells us, for example, that at the time of the French Union, Laye had written a text in which he proposed "that the best way to establish the French Union on a firm foundation would be to arrange a regular exchange of children between metropolitan France and the colonies: 'A new brotherhood of spirit . . . will be born more easily as the child gives his friendship more readily, is more confident and without prejudices . . . The future of l'Union Française is in the hands of youth.' "[7] This idealistic vision is typical of the author's thinking, which is certainly more that of a poet than a politician. Love of God, friendship, and good will are qualities that Laye believed essential to good government and the happiness of humanity. His political naiveté and his moderation were irritating to some of the younger writers of his generation, and were perhaps taken for a lack of political courage at a time when the majority of African intellectuals felt they were the spokesmen of their race, and the purpose of writing was to liberate themselves and their people.

By the early 1950s in any event, Laye was a celebrity on both continents, and a happily married man (he had married Marie Lorofi in Paris in 1953). But although life was now easy and pleasant, Laye had difficulties in accepting the materialism of French society. For the author, true France was elsewhere, in its art, its architecture, and the beauty of its language. Advanced technology did not impress him so much as artistic and intellectual achievements, and by the same token, he felt that Africa, which totally lacked technology, still had a lot to contribute to the world. His thinking is in keeping with his preoccupation with traditional African culture, and explains his life-long devotion to the compilation and preservation of the oral litera-ture of his Malinké culture. His definition of civilization did not change with time, and in the preface to his last book he wrote:

> Civilization is perhaps a way of doing things, a style of living . . . And civilization existed before the industrial age, before the technical progress which resulted from it; this progress, Africa does not refuse it, on the con-trary, she is impatiently awaiting it, but she regards it and should wisely continue to regard it as complementary to civilization itself.[8]

The French Political Context

After World War II, the relationship between France and its col-onies began to change. The French constitution of 1946 included a new plan for the French Union, the government of the overseas ter-ritories. It emphasized equality of rights and obligations. All inhab-itants of the French colonies were declared French citizens, which meant that they were entitled to representation in the French Na-tional Assembly. This new representation brought many African de-puties and representatives to France, where they learned the intri-cacies of the parliamentary system. They influenced the colonial educational system, and most likely gave their constituents a sense of identity which would come into play in the granting of independ-ence. By 1954, several French governments had had African minis-ters: Senghor, Houphouët-Boigny, and Modibo Keita to name but a few. Other important reforms brought about by the fourth Republic were the abolition of forced labor and the adoption of the French penal code for Africans. In 1952, new labor laws were enacted which considerably liberalized the activities of African unions, which had gained the right to organize in 1944.

African labor unions played an important political and social role in the development of their countries and the play for independence. Sekou Touré, for example, the current president of Guinea, rose to power from the union movement and the 1947–48 dramatic strike of the workers of the Dakar-Niger, immortalized by the Senegalese writer Ousmane Sembene in his novel *Les Bouts de bois de Dieu* (1960), was responsible for the establishment of the labor code. Finally, in 1956, Gaston Deferre's "loi cadre" (enabling act) for French West and Equatorial Africa brought a new dimension to the political situation. The most important part of the law was its

provision for the devolution of the legislative powers to the individual territorial assemblies from the French National Assembly . . . In essence the basic political relationship would be between the French Republic and the individual territory. The balkanization of French Black Africa that would result was opposed by Sekou Touré.[9]

This was one of the reasons for his refusal to participate in De Gaulle's French Community, proposed in 1958.

Les Soleils des Indépendances[10]

In 1945, the political scene in Guinea was dominated by four indigenous parties representing the four main ethnic groups and their regions. In 1946, at the instigation of African deputies elected to the French Assembly, a general conference of African leaders at which Sekou Touré was one of the Guinean delegates was held in Bamako, Mali, in order to formulate a common policy for French Black Africa. This was the beginning of the RDA (Rassemblement Démocratique Africain). Later on, the Guinean branch of the RDA was formed under the name of the Democratic Party of Guinea (PDG). In 1952, Sekou Touré became secretary general of the PDG and recruited members from the labor unions affiliated with the largest French labor union, the CGT (Confédération Générale du Travail). A year later, Touré secured a seat in the territorial assembly, thus demonstrating his ability to win rural votes as his popularity increased. His ambition was to reach the French National Assembly, and in the 1954 elections his main opponent was Diawedou Barry, the head of the African Bloc of Guinea (BAG), a conservative party backed by the white residents. Touré lost and claimed corruption and irregularities. The PDG continued its campaign, and since its program was mostly directed toward the masses, the peasant class, and women, it won a huge following, enabling it to take two of the three seats in the French Assembly in 1956. Sekou Touré was one of the deputies elected. The passing of the Loi-Cadre gave new importance to the Territorial Assembly and the PDG concentrated its efforts on controlling it. To broaden its membership, it reduced the importance of intellectuals, once more directing its appeal to the masses and becoming the party of the people. Little by little, it secured more power, pushing for reforms and Africanization of the government and administration. By the time of De Gaulle's referendum, the PDG, with Sekou Touré as its leader, was in complete control of Guinean politics.

In 1958, the "non" of Sekou Touré was heard like a shot in the French community. De Gaulle's referendum for or against the French Community, a new association between France and its colonies, obtained an overwhelming majority, and Guinea was the only dissenter. De Gaulle had stated that a "No" would automatically result in independence and all its consequences—namely, of course, the severance of most economic and technical ties with France. On 2 October 1958, Guinea became an independent republic. De Gaulle kept his word and cut off aid, and most French technicians left the country. In 1959, agreements were signed between France and its former colony establishing diplomatic representation, acceptance of French as the official language, and the retention of Guinea in the French Franc zone; relations were strained, however, and broken in 1965, to be renewed ten years later.[11]

Camara Laye and his wife had gone back to Africa in 1956, first to Dahomey (now called Bénin) and then to Ghana. After independence, Laye went back home to participate in the establishment of the new republic, but he did not stay in the country for very long. He was the first ambassador to Ghana and was "instrumental in obtaining Ghanian aid when French assistance was cut off."[12] He subsequently held a number of government posts outside the country, and finally went back to Conakry to be in charge of the Department of Economic Agreements (accords économiques) for the Ministry of Foreign Affairs. He then became an editor attached to the presidency, and from 1963 to 1965 he was associate director of the National Institute of Research and Documentation. While occupying these official posts, Laye had started to gather material on the oral tradition of the Manding, and interviewed and recorded several legends. He consulted many griots, who are the genealogists, storytellers, and traditionalists of West Africa. He began his session with the griot Babou Condé and gathered the basic material for his last book, *Le Maître de la parole.* He was also writing plays for Radio-Conakry which were broadcast weekly, on Sunday morning. One of the plays is incorporated in his third book, *Dramouss,* as the Griot's Tale. In 1957, he had published a short story, "Les yeux de la statue," followed by an article, "Et Demain?", on urban living, both in *Présence Africaine.*

As a well-known writer, his work had begun to be analyzed and acclaimed in African literary reviews such as *Black Orpheus* and *Présence Africaine,* and he was anthologized in all the major studies on African literature. In 1963, he participated in the conference on African literature, both anglophone and francophone, held at the University of Dakar, Senegal, and a month later at Fourah Bay College in Freetown, Sierra Leone. In Dakar, Laye talked about "L'Âme de l'Afrique dans sa partie guinéenne," in which he explained the genesis of *L'Enfant noir;* while in Freetown, his subject was "L'Afrique et l'appel des profondeurs," which he illustrated by telling of a dream he had experienced, the dream of the Black Lion, which he would later use in *Dramouss.* The papers of the two conferences were published in 1965, edited by the critic Gerald Moore, who remarks in his introduction:

A common presence at both conferences was the quiet radiant personality of Camara Laye. Both his contributions are preserved here, for they were the uniquely creative fruits of our meeting, the first full of autobiographical detail and the second illustrating in a very interesting fashion the writer's method of symbolic elaboration of ideas, ideas which he sees and can present in no other form. [13]

It is evident that by the early 1960s, Laye's career was on the upswing and he was becoming more and more successful both as an artist and as a government official. This situation was to alter drastically as Sekou Touré's regime took a turn toward dictatorship. After independence, the Guinean government found itself hard pressed financially but thought it could offset the lack of funds by tapping its human resources. Enthusiasm and good will toward the new Republic were great, and people did not seem to mind working for next to nothing if it helped the country. But by the 1960s, many difficulties had begun to appear and public enthusiasm had started to wane. It is not possible here to give a complete account of the complex situation in Guinea, or to explain Touré's regime, but it is generally accepted that soon after independence the Guinean regime gave evidence of living in fear of an internal eruption. It feared a political coup, and many alleged and real plots were uncovered followed by the usual purges and repression. Sekou Touré accused foreign powers of being the instigators of the plots, and of trying to sabotage the "revolution." However, it is well known that many were staged by Guinean dissidents. In 1965, Guinea severed diplomatic ties with France following the so-called "Traders' plot" (complot des commerçants), allegedly fomented by the French government.[14]

Laye had been dissatisfied with the regime for some time, not only because he did not agree with some of Touré's ideas but because he realized that the regime was turning into a dictatorship and a bloody one at that. Using ill health as a pretext, he obtained permission to leave the country and left with his family for Dakar in 1965. With him he had the manuscript of *Dramouss,* published in 1966 in Paris, in which he expresses his discontent with Sekou Touré's regime. Laye was one of the first to become disenchanted with the Guinean revolution and to denounce it. His opposition was to be substantiated fully in the years to come, with numerous individual testimonies, like the controversial book by Jean-Paul Alata, *Prison d'Afrique* (1976), and the Canadian film *La Danse avec l'aveugle* (1978),[15] exposing the atrocities of the sinister "camp Boiro," one of Sekou Touré's worst prison camps.

Political exile brought tragedy into Camara Laye's life. In Dakar, he was given a position at the IFAN (Institut Fondamental d'Afrique Noire), but his financial situation became strained, and it became more and more difficult to support his seven children. His financial plight did not ease with time, and was a source of distress until the end of his life. In Dakar, he continued his work with oral traditions, and often left the city for several days to go into the villages to listen to the griots of various regions such as Guinea-Bissau and Casamance, in southern Senegal.

In 1970, his wife, Marie, received a cable, presumably from friends, stating that her father, who had just been released from prison, was very ill and desperate to see her. Despite Laye's uneasiness about her returning to Guinea, she decided to go; she was seized at the airport upon arrival and imprisoned for seven years—because she was Laye's wife. Meanwhile, the author was left alone to care for his seven children; he married a young Senegalese woman, Ramatoulaye Kanté, by whom he had three more children. In 1975, he became very ill with a kidney infection (hypertensive nephritis) and was hospitalized in Dakar. It soon became evident that specialized treatment was needed, and that he would have to go to Paris if he were to survive, but this was financially out of the question for him.

Reine Carducci, granddaughter of the academician René Grousset and wife of the Italian ambassador to UNESCO in Senegal, became aware of Camara Laye's plight and launched an appeal throughout Europe, by means of radio and the press, to raise funds to pay for "l'enfant noir" 's medical expenses. In France, Mrs. Carducci contacted Jean Blanzat, one of Laye's first admirers, and with the help of Jean d'Ormesson, Pierre Emmanuel, Dimitri Stoleypin, president of the P.E.N. club, and many others, an appeal was launched to inform the public. At the same time, Plon, Laye's publisher, reprinted all of his work, which brought in a considerable sum in royalties. F. Houphouët-Boigny, President of the Ivory Coast and a friend of Laye, contributed enormously to the fund, and thus Laye was able to go to Paris, where he was successfully treated at the Necker Hospital.

Besides saving his life, the appeal brought him the satisfaction of knowing that his public had not forgotten him, and that he belonged to the international community of literature. Many letters came from children, because L'Enfant noir was taught in French schools, and Laye was very touched by the responses. For a couple of years, his financial worries subsided, and in 1978 he published his last work, Le Maître de la parole, dedicated to Mrs. Carducci, who had truly saved his life and made his last years easier by her kindness and concern.[16] In 1977, Marie had been released from prison thanks to an appeal to Sekou Touré in which Mrs. Carducci had also played a role. However, Marie was unable to accept Laye's second wife and filed for divorce.

During his stay in Senegal, Laye had written a novel called L'Exil and in 1971 he informed Plon that he had completed the manuscript. Besides being an attack on the Guinean regime, the book contained some sensitive political material which could have been damaging to Laye and his family; consequently he was advised not to publish it; he did not. He was much concerned by the political situation in his homeland and was actively involved in the opposition movement to Sekou Touré. He was in contact with opposing groups in France, Africa, and the United States. He saw Sekou Touré as an evil man leading the country to ruin, and he hoped to see him fall in the near future. Many of his friends and former colleagues had either been jailed or executed, and it was public knowledge that the regime was repressive, although the world community did not appear to care.

Laye did not approve of the renewal of diplomatic ties between France and Guinea, since that meant a tacit acceptance of Touré's regime, and he also felt that the OUA (Organisation de l'Unité Africaine) should have taken a stand and censured the violation of human rights prevailing in his homeland. It is ironic that despite his reputation as a moderate and an independent, Laye was deeply political. His interest in the affairs of Guinea and the African continent in general had been present since his student years, and never waned. His private papers indicate that not only was he struggling to bring down the Guinean regime, but that he was prepared to play a key role in the government to come.[17] And yet, his literary output hardly reflects his political interest and involvement. He kept the two activities separate, and, as he grew more active in contemporary problems, he seemed to be more and more drawn to the cultural past of Africa and its traditional oral genres.

However, his intellectual and creative pursuits were as active as his political interests. In 1970, he published an article, "The Black Man and Arts," in *African Arts,* in which he insists upon the religious origin of African art. In 1972, he went to London to participate in the International Conference on Manding Studies and he delivered a lecture on the importance of dreams in traditional Malinké society. For a while he did research on the Almamy Samory Touré, the last of the great Sudanese conquerers, who, by the end of the nineteenth century, had set up a vast empire and successfully resisted the French invasions for many years. Laye wanted to do a doctoral thesis on the Almamy but gave up the project because Professor Yves Person's study on the subject was a definitive work and Laye felt he could not add anything new to the matter. Moreover, he had many other projects in preparation, one of them being a work on Houphouët-Boigny, about which he went so far as to contact his publisher, Plon. The title of the work was to be "Felix Houphouët-Boigny Kouma," which seems to imply that the president of the Ivory Coast would be the protagonist of a modern epic, as Kouma (which means "the Word" in Malinké) is used to indicate the history of contemporary man. Laye had also approached an old griot, with whom he had frequent contacts, to compose the saga of the RDA (Réssemblement Démocratique Africain), which he would then transcribe into French. It appears from these projects that the author sought to continue the epic tradition into modern times, to immortalize for future generations the modern African leaders for whom he had respect. He was in the process of gathering folk tales for children when the old illness flared up again and death put an abrupt end to all his plans. Camara Laye died in exile on 4 February 1980 in Dakar, where he is buried.

Chapter Two
L'Enfant noir

Introduction

Although published thirteen years apart, *L'Enfant noir* (The Dark Child) and *Dramouss* constitute an autobiographical entity, a double-headed mask representing the past and the future more as a continuum than in opposition. These books are an exploration of Malinké culture and an affirmation that its values are able to withstand not only the erosion of time, but the dramatic changes imposed on them by Western culture, technology, and aborted revolutions. In valorizing this past, Camara Laye is in fact looking toward the future and hoping for a new world harmoniously linked with the old. The vision of a new world in *Dramouss* is expressed primarily through the symbolic imagery of *L'Enfant noir*, imagery which is rooted in the ancient world of the father and the mother, recaptured and reconstituted by the author's own sensibility and imagination.

L'Enfant noir, which Camara Laye had wanted to call *The Guinean Child*, originated as a form of relief from the author's loneliness and home-sickness:

Living in Paris, far from my native Guinea, far from my parents, having lived there for years in rarely interrupted isolation, I bore myself in thought a thousand times to my country, close to my people . . . and then, one day, I thought that these memories, which at this time were still fresh, could with time, if not fade away—how could they ever fade away?—lose their strength, and then I began to write. I was living alone, alone in my poor student room, and I was writing. I was writing as one dreams; I was remembering; I was writing for the pleasure of it; and it was an extraordinary pleasure, a pleasure forever pleasing to the heart.[1]

Thus was born *L'Enfant noir*, for the benefit of the heart, for the pleasure of it, and not as an artistic endeavor. It was a friend who, having read the material, convinced Camara Laye to work on his style and to present the manuscript to a publisher. The literary merits of the book are undeniable and reveal a born writer, but it is the spontaneity and sincerity of the content which have charmed its readers. This book of remembrance is not an introspection into childhood in order to discover oneself. The hero of the book is in fact not "the black child" but rather Africa and its values, which Eric Sellin calls "Laye's fictional alter-ego."[2]

It is one of the ever-changing forces of Africa that Camara Laye is trying to recapture, to understand. It is not a sociological account of life in a Guinean village (although there is some of that, and this greatly contributed to the immediate success of the book), but a poetic and subjective vision of the motherland, its beauty, its mysteries, and its intangible spirit. It is an idyllic portrait of Malinké culture, and as such it sounded a false note in the ironic and bitter African fiction of the 1950s, which at the time was concerned primarily with the struggle for independence and the psychological trauma of colonialism.

Although *L'Enfant noir* is situated in colonial times, the white man is absent from the book. His presence is felt only indirectly as an element of change through that most ambiguous and powerful manifestation of his presence: the school. The future belongs to those with a Western education and, in the case of the Dark Child, a French education. He will therefore learn to speak, to write, and to think in French, but Malinké will remain the language of the heart. Labeled as a disciple of Négritude, Camara Laye was nevertheless one of the few francophone writers to be at peace with his hybrid culture. He was in fact a francophile, and thought French colonialism had not been totally negative. He had no identity problem, and never lost touch either with his upbringing or with the original Malinké values according to which he had been raised. He did not object to being a Frenchman, but he was proud to be an African. He used his French education to serve his African culture, and it was in French that he spoke to us of Africa.

Laye has a timeless vision of Africa in the sense that it always focuses on the spiritual content of the image and its essential values; the author's own historical context is thus not given the attention that most African intellectuals feel it deserves, and indeed which it usually receives in African fiction. For Laye, whose universe is dominated by the divine, it seems that the historical context is secondary, merely a fleeting and accidental moment masking the true reality of culture under an array of facts and objects. The importance of Ma-

linké culture lies not in how it was and is being transformed by the
West, but in how its intrinsic values are surviving. *L'Enfant noir*
could have been written at almost any time; as autobiographical fiction, it is indeed timeless. What appealed to the European public was
both the familiarity of the theme and the exoticism of the subject.
No African had ever written such an account before, in such good
French, with such detail on the ceremonies and mysteries of the so-
called Dark Continent.

The book was an immediate success and unanimously praised by
European critics. A year after its publication, in 1954, it received the
Charles Veillon prize.[3] To understand how Western critics perceived
the work is to understand the controversy that it raised among the
African intelligentsia. The French critic Jean Blanzat wrote in *Le Fi-
garo Littéraire,*

> How does Camara Laye experience a metamorphosis which began in 1945
> and which is coming to an end? Is he torn between two different universes?
> How does he judge the one in which he has been raised, and of which he
> necessarily knows the singularity and the limits? What is he retaining from
> it and what is he rejecting? Here is, undoubtedly, the single most surprising
> element of the book. For Camara Laye, these questions do not exist. He
> trusts the whites, but none of the knowledge he has gotten from them
> touches his inner life. He feels no intellectual anguish. His cultural integ-
> rity is total. He does not feel separated from his people by an inner distance,
> but only by geographical space. His mind does not choose or reject any-
> thing: he keeps everything, because if the spirit has changed it has also re-
> mained the same. The testimony of Camara Laye shows how, in an extreme
> case, the heart resolves the problem: by ignoring it![4]

That he ignored it is exactly what many African intellectuals held
against Laye. They read into it an unbelievable indifference to the
drama of colonialism, and saw his lack of anguish as a lack of com-
mitment. The Camerounean writer Mongo Beti launched the most
severe attack on the book and the author. Although he represented
the most extreme criticism, he expressed forcefully a more nuanced
but general discontent.

In his celebrated critique, published in *Présence Africaine* in 1954,
Beti expressed his disappointment and dismay at the "monstrous ab-
sence of vision and depth in the Guinean's book."[5] He compared
L'Enfant noir with Richard Wright's *Black Boy,* and drew the obvious
conclusion that Laye presented an idyllic and therefore false image of

Africa and deliberately closed his eyes to unpleasant reality. As for the descriptions of village life and ceremonies which so enchanted the European readers, Beti dismissed them as nothing more than snapshot journalism worthy of the more sensational magazines. Moderation is not Beti's forte, and however exaggerated and unfair his criticism was, it did succeed in making Laye's political integrity somewhat suspect in the African world of letters. At best, he was considered a *naïf,* a considerable talent surely, but not quite in the mainstream, not quite one of the group. This suspicion was aroused by each of his published works, although it was to lessen in time.

As the controversy abated, critics began to explore *L'Enfant noir* as a work of art, and criticism took on a more literary turn. However, the old suspicion remained in the background and appeared in filigree in many of the major studies of the book, often taking the form of a defense of the author's political stand. For example, Paul Edwards and Kenneth Ramchand, writing in 1970, declared: "In this article we want to show that the *African Child* is committed to an anticolonial line on the level of cultural polemics."[6] Ironically, their main reticence about the book comes from the fact that they saw in Laye's work an unfair criticism of European civilization in the Rousseauist manner, thus explaining its idealized portrayal of African village life. Interestingly enough, Laye neither defended nor justified his political stand, or alleged lack of one. He had written the book he had to write in order to satisfy his yearning to capture a vanishing world. The Guinea described in *L'Enfant noir* was his Guinea, the one he had experienced and, more important, the one he remembered. If his Africa did not resemble that of some of his contemporaries, it made no difference. One cannot adjust one's vision to fit the times and still be true to oneself.

It is of course evident that the controversy over the book was more a question of timing than content. If it were to be published today, it would hardly be controversial. In fact, a Rwandan intellectual, Christophe Mfizi, commenting on *L'Enfant noir* in 1971, reflects the changing African attitude toward Laye and his work. When asked why he took Laye's work as the subject of his doctoral thesis, he answered: "I chose Laye Camara first because I had liked *L'Enfant noir.* It said what I would have liked to say, what I was feeling after two years in Belgium. I saw myself in *L'Enfant noir.*"[7] As for the author's politics, Mfizi considers it an irrelevant question. There can be no denying that Laye had a conservative temperament, nor can there be any doubt that he was also totally committed to the affirmation of the African spirit and its values.

On a more properly literary and artistic level, the critics have for the most part grudgingly conceded that *L'Enfant noir* is a minor masterpiece. The book is easily divided into two parts: the first eight chapters deal specifically with life in Kouroussa and the author's life up to the age of fifteen, and the last four tell of his life as a student in Conakry, his emotional attachment to Marie, and his departure for France. Most critics agree that the last four chapters of the book are the weakest, and that, as Eustace Palmer puts it, "The appeal of *The African Child* largely derives from Camara Laye's powerful portrayal of traditional life . . . The reason why excerpts from [the book] are found frequently in anthologies is that it is made up of a number of self-contained episodes together forming a coherent picture of a dignified society."[8] In addition, Adèle King believes that "despite the African setting, the picture of childhood and adolescence in *L'Enfant noir* is timeless and universal . . . It belongs to a tradition of novels concerned with the process of growing up and moving beyond the security of the family."[9] Lilyan Kesteloot's view that "c'est une réussite de style,"[10] reminds us of the criterion by which the literary value of any book must be judged, a criterion which is all too often overlooked in the appraisal of African literature. *L'Enfant noir* has the quality of its faults, and if it is sometimes sentimental and naive, it also possesses great sincerity of feeling and a fresh, poetic vision of life. It is the book of a young man, of an inexperienced but very promising writer whose images come from the imagination of the heart.

The first-person narrative brings a sincere and intimate quality to the book. It is for the most part written in the imperfect tense, except for the ceremony of "Kondén Diara," which is narrated largely in the present to make it more vivid and more real. The imperfect tense, being in French the tense of past narration, suits the autobiographical theme well. Since it is also a tense which insists on the duration of the action of the verb, rather than simply stating that an action has taken place, it thus situates it specifically in time. According to Senghor, "Negro-African languages insist on the notion of aspect, which means that they are essentially concrete."[11] He goes on to say that, in African languages, words are always generating images, surrealist images in which the object does not signify what it represents but rather what it suggests, what it creates. In *L'Enfant noir,* Laye uses images as symbols or ideograms; for example, the little black snake which appears regularly to his father is more than just a snake, it is the spirit of the race, which later reappears in *Dramouss* as a big black snake with a slightly different meaning. Moreover, Laye's images are reinforced by the repetitive rhythm that vitalizes the author's sentence structure.[12]

Remembrance

Looking toward his past, the author is struck by the things he did not understand. Everyday life in Kouroussa, the trip to his grandmother's house, the family, the games with the other village boys, even the ceremony of circumcision are events he remembers with fondness and warmth, since they pertain to a happy childhood and attest to the sweetness of life as it used to be, as well as contribute to a nostalgia for time past. But what truly fascinates him is the mass of events he witnessed without comprehending their full meaning, or without being able to explain how they could have taken place. This fascination is, as it were, after the fact, the product of a Western education, of exile, of aging. The grown man living in Paris, thinking and writing about old times, suddenly realizes that a large part of his childhood has escaped him. Explaining his yearning, he writes, "My whole being cries out for wonders, for prodigies, and when I recognize their presence I know that it is the better part of myself awakening, my whole self."[13] It is like trying to decipher a particularly vivid, pleasant, but cryptic dream that one has had repeatedly, without ever understanding its meaning. Those who hold the keys to the obscure dream are his parents, since they are the last link to an old order of things where he, Camara Laye, is only a witness and no longer a participant.

This essay will explore exclusively the first eight chapters of the book insofar as they are dominated by the dual vision of Malinké culture and of the hero's parents, thereby allowing us a glimpse into that ancient world which is the object of the author's quest and the source of his art. However, the ceremony of the lions (Kondén Diara) and the ritual of circumcision, which Laye recalls in much detail in these first chapters, will be omitted from this study, since they are primarily recollections of concrete ritualistic events. Kondén Diara, during which small boys are terrorized by the roaring of always invisible lions, is a mystification, as the author later discovers, and as such did not fire his imagination with lasting images discernible in his art. Similarly, the ceremony of circumcision, although vividly reported and recalled, is perceived as an important but traditional and predictable cultural experience in the life of a young Malinké boy. There are no mysteries attached to it, no unresolved questions, and therefore no fascination, but simply the remembrance of time past.

Camara Laye's recollection of his past begins with the world of his father, who was a blacksmith and a goldsmith as well as the head of the extended Camara family, Malinké culture being patrilineal. He is remembered essentially for what he represents in the context of ancient Africa. We know very little of the father as a man, except that he was good and righteous, well liked, and respected by all. The glowing paternal image is exceptional in francophone African literature, where the father is usually a detestable, selfish, and tyrannical individual, standing for everything that is wrong with tradition. Laye sees his father as the living symbol of an ancient culture inexorably doomed by history. Whatever the reason, the author's obsession for his Malinké heritage is evident and constant throughout his work, and *The Dark Child* is a spontaneous cry of love and anguish, an attempt to halt destruction through the use of the most powerful tool man has ever invented for himself: the written word. This single book contains the essential symbolic imagery that will reoccur throughout the author's entire work.

The Father's World

Of his father's world, Camara Laye remembers first and foremost the little black snake which visited his father regularly. As a child, his first encounter with snakes resembled that of most children. He was taught to fear them, to stay away from them, and when possible to kill them. But his experience becomes highly personal as he comes to realize that there is an exception to this otherwise rigid rule, and this exception is the little black snake. This snake, his mother informs him, must not be harmed and need not be feared since "it is the guiding spirit of your father . . . although I was familiar with the supernatural, I remained speechless, so great was my astonishment."[14] The little black snake transforms the father into an exceptional being, a surreal character at ease in two worlds, the supernatural world being visibly and for all to know an undeniable part of his father's life.

Although the child's mother is considered a witch, the father is not a sorcerer; he simply knows and understands what lies beyond so-called reality. He engages in daily rituals and uses magic potions, for what purpose the child does not, and never will, know, but guesses that the rituals and potions are protecting his father against possible evil. The existence of spirits, good and bad, is an everyday reality in ancient Africa and, as everywhere else, there are more evil spirits than good ones. For the child, the presence of the little snake transfigures the image of the father as that of a chosen individual to whom the spirits speak directly, and as the son of such a father, he feels proud and special.

He feels that the presence of the snake is men's business in which women have no part, and therefore he waits until evening, the proper time to talk about such things. Alone with his father, he asks him about the little black snake. "That snake," says the father, "is the guiding spirit of our race. Can you understand that? . . . that snake is always present: he always appears to one of us. In our generation, it is to me that he has appeared . . . he first appeared in the semblance of a dream."[15] The father continues that all he has and all he is he owes "to the snake, I owe it to the guiding spirit of our race."[16] Finally he adds, ". . . but it is true however that if you want to inherit it in your turn, you will have to conduct yourself in the selfsame manner [as I]; from now on, it will be necessary for you to be more and more in my company."[17]

This is the first and last conversation the child has with his father on the subject of the snake. To know more, he needs to stay in his father's company, but instead he goes to the white man's school. The unfinished lesson was to haunt Camara Laye all his life, and cause him to go further and further into the past in search of ancient wisdom and knowledge.

As a symbol, the snake is not rare in Western Africa. It can be a cosmogonic symbol, as it is for the Dogon and the Bambara, or the protecting god of a nation, as in Togo and Dahomey. It often plays a totemic role; one thinks of the sacred python of Samory the conqueror. Finally it is frequently a symbol of fecundity, as for the Bamileke. In Laye's story the symbol is clearly spelled out, but the actual choice of symbol is not explained, although it would seem to have a totemic significance due to the close relationship between the father and the animal; as J. E. Cirlot points out in his *Dictionary of Symbols,* ". . . in the world of symbols, totemistic interpretation does no more than demonstrate relationship, without elucidating meaning: it forges connecting links between beings endowed with 'common rhythm,' but it does not indicate the meaning of these beings."[18] Laye never explains why the spirit of the father is symbolized by a little black snake rather than some other animal form.

The father was chosen to receive the guiding spirit of the race because of his behavior, which was considered worthy, and also because of his trade, which is a sacred one in ancient Africa; we shall return to this matter later. The father had been warned of the honor bestowed upon him in true Malinké fashion, through a premonitory dream, which he had not understood at first; as a result, he had reacted with fear in the presence of the snake. But when the dream comes a second time, the father understands and accepts his destiny, and his fear vanishes. He knows then that he has become a link between the natural and the supernatural world, that he is in harmony with the cosmic forces that control the universe. He knows that the ordinary things around us are not what they seem, that they contain power and knowledge which are sometimes revealed to the few who are worthy of knowing. He believes, as his ancestors had believed, and has been chosen to attest to the fact that the visible world is but a small part of the true world, and that one does not need to understand in order to believe.

The son shares his father's faith, but not his knowledge. Laye mentions several times that he saw, as a child, phenomena he could not explain as a rational, educated man, and yet he saw them. But because he was so young and left his father's side too soon, he was only a witness and would never be more than that. In the old order of things, he could have been the true heir to his father, and in his turn be the chosen one, the one who is initiated into the secrets which are at the root of the tradition. ". . . I should have liked, I should have liked so much that it be my turn to place my hand on the snake, that it be my turn to understand and listen to that tremor, but I was not sure of how the snake would receive my hand and I did not feel that it had anything to tell me; I feared it would never have anything to tell me."[19]

But, as a witness, he can testify to what he has seen, even if some of its meaning escapes him; and, as an artist, he can impose a new order in which he is the chosen one. Unable to decipher the cryptic message of the ancient world, a prisoner of tangible reality which constitutes only half the truth, Laye uses the supernatural manifestations of his father's world to symbolize his own ideal and his vision of the future as it will be found in *Dramouss,* for example. But in *L'Enfant noir* he simply remembers, and lets his imagination wander among the marvels of his parents' world. If the little black snake is an avatar of the supernatural, the intangible, the unattainable, the father's workshop on the other hand is at the core of the author's creativity, for it represents the magic of creation, where the Dark Child will not remain an outsider, but will become a true participant.

In many African cultures, as in other ancient civilizations, the blacksmith was a very important figure. He was, as Senghor calls him, the polytechnician of magic and art. He often presided over, and participated in, the rites of puberty and circumcision, and had a role in most secret societies. Frequently, as in the case of Camara Laye's father, he was also a goldsmith and a sculptor, i.e., an artist. Malinké society being clanic, the smith belongs to a clan related to his trade, which sets him apart in his society, in which he holds a privileged and sometimes feared position. He is, to quote Mircea Eliade, "the main agent for the transmission of mythologies, rites and metallurgical mysteries."[20] The Dark Child's father is familiar with these metallurgical mysteries, and his knowledge is never more evident than when he works with gold.

Gold has had extraordinary spiritual importance in the history of man. To quote Eliade once again, "Gold was the first metal to be discovered and used by man, although it was used neither as a tool nor as a weapon. In the history of technological evolution, stone, bronze, iron, steel, gold played no part."[21] The noble metal has always been worked by man for religious, spiritual, and aesthetic purposes; the ancient hermetic pursuit of the alchemists, which is usually traced to the Egyptian and later to the Arab world, attests to the predominantly spiritual atmosphere which surrounds the working of gold. As in most archaic civilizations, the working and the symbolism of gold in most African cultures take on ritual and religious significance. The smelting of gold belongs to a universal phase of human development and thinking, even if it occurs at different times for different civilizations, and this phase belongs to what Eliade calls symbolic thinking: "To symbolic thinking the world is not only 'alive' but also 'open': an object is never simply itself (as is the case in modern consciousness), it is also a sign of, or a repository for, something else."[22] Thus, the portrayal of Laye's father is an excellent example of symbolic thinking.

An entire chapter is dedicated to the father as a goldsmith, and the author relates an incident which happened fairly often. A woman asks the father to make her a piece of jewelry out of some gold dust she has extracted herself from the mud of the river. To put the goldsmith in a receptive mood, so he will not only agree to make the piece, but to do it right away, the woman brings a griot as a go-between. The griot installed himself in the workshop and "tuned up his cora, which is our harp, and began to sing my father's praises."[23] The father is not insensitive to the flattery of the griot, and he lends a favorable ear to the exploits and wonderful achievements of his ancestors and basks in their glory, which is his also. There occurs a softening and mellowing of the smith's habitual sternness, for he is being prepared to respond to the woman's wish. She is very eager, and, to use Laye's word, "desire" lies behind her eagerness, desire for a beautiful gold ornament which she will wear proudly during the next holiday.

In a typically African misogynist portrayal of woman as morally weak, vain, superficial, and overly preoccupied with her appearance, she is shown as lusting after the piece of jewelry. But the woman's concupiscence is further brought out to infuse the scene with sensual and even sexual overtones, although it is clear that the ambient sexuality does not refer to, or imply, anything illicit between the father and his client. Rather, the woman's desire for the gold piece sets the mood for ritual and symbolic sexuality, which is usually inferred in archaic gold or metal smelting. The smelting of the ore has been compared to the sexual act in the sense that it is a creative act whereby man interferes directly with cosmic forces such as wind and fire, inducing them to transgress the earth's temporal rhythm and to accelerate the normal gestation and maturation of the metal. By this forcible marriage, he not only imposes his will on form but also on time, transforming, as Eliade says, geological time into vital time. But man can do this only with the compliance of the genies and spirits of fire and wind, and he must win their approval, just as the woman has won his. The smith is not only a craftsman and an artist, but also and most importantly a priest, a translator, and a manipulator of supernatural powers and vital energies. To secure the success of his project, he must know and follow the ancient rituals which have been passed on to him since time immemorial:

The craftsman who works with gold must first purify himself; he must wash himself all over, and, of course, abstain from all sexual commerce during the whole period of the operation. Great respecter of ceremony as he was, it would have been impossible for my father to ignore these rules. Now, I never saw him retiring to his hut. I saw him harness himself to his task without any apparent preliminaries. Consequently, it was obvious that, forewarned in a dream by his black guiding spirit, my father must have prepared for the task ahead as soon as he arose, entering his workshop in a state of purity.[24]

The ritual purity which is demanded of the father emphasizes the spiritual value attached to gold smelting, as well as the symbolic union of the elements which is to take place protected from all human impurities, so as not to offend the elemental spirits. Laye describes the fusion of the gold in religious and connubial terms. The operation is done in silence, under the respectful eyes of the apprentices, the griot, and the child, stimulated by the soundless incantations of the celebrant. Only the elemental spirits speak as they are blending their energies to comply with the prayers and conjurations of the smith, calling for the union of wind, fire, and gold. The child remembers the voices of the elements, "the silence was broken only by the panting of the bellows and the faint whistle of the gold."[25] It is the sound of mating, the successful consummation of the elemental marriage, and, once the gold has liquified, the father breaks the silence to mark that the first step toward the making of the ornament is now complete.

Although the child is fascinated by the ritual of gold smelting and the mysterious forces it unleashes, it is the father as artist who seems the more glorious in his eyes. As he prepares himself to stretch and hammer the cooled gold, the father caresses the little black snake to gather strength for the most trying part of his task. The goldsmith will now display his skill and imagination. The whole workshop watches beauty in the making, particularly the woman, who has come to look on in great expectation. Unlike the smelting of the gold, the creation of the ornament is undertaken in loud joy and excitement. The griot's music increases in tempo and praise for the artist, thus giving a sonorous account of the progression of the work and its worth. The woman's eyes are "devouring the fragile gold wire" as she watches intensely the concretization of her desire. The goldsmith's creation is like a birth, a joyous communal event, a spectacle, a "fête," where the audience can appreciate and participate in the skill and the talent of the artist in the process of creation. This public attention is usually reserved for no other artist but the goldsmith, adding therefore to his prestige and the nobility of his craft. Slowly, the piece takes shape, comes into being, under the skillful and precise manipulation of the father. From a handful of dust, from shapelessness, he has extracted form, order, and beauty; he has imposed his will on matter. The griot, as a fellow artist, is most moved by this spectacle:

He was no longer a hired censer-bearer, he was no longer this man whose services anyone could rent. He was a man who created his song out of some deep inner necessity. And when my father, after having soldered the large grain of gold that crowned the summit, held out his work to be admired, the praise singer was no longer able to contain himself from intoning the "douga," the great chant which is sung only for celebrated men and which is danced by them alone. [26]

But, as the author explains, the douga is a dangerous dance and one must protect oneself before dancing. The father and the griot have taken the necessary precautions against the evil spirits that the dance provokes and releases. The douga is reserved for men of deeds. The father, the artist, dances his accomplishment, his creation, his joy, his pride. He is attracting attention to himself and opening himself to be hurt by evil and jealous forces which are always present and waiting for a vulnerable moment. One does not create without risk, but one does not create without rewards either. [27] The goldsmith has smelted the gold with the help and protection of the supernatural, with which he has been in contact through his knowledge of the ancestral rituals and through his lineage. In doing so he has traveled smoothly and naturally from the sacred to the temporal, the ideal to the tangible; he has transformed dust into solid matter, thus reversing the process of destruction. He has become a man of deeds who has given form to chaos, harmonizing his creative rhythm with the rhythm of the cora, the rhythm of the griot's words. Laye insists on the intermingling of the music and the creation of the ornament, on the two artists working in harmony, transported by the same rhythmic forces, the griot being like a midwife who helps in the birthing. For them, the created piece is more than a simple ornament, it is the wondrous concretization of cosmic rhythms.

For the author, the father, dancing the douga is like a magnificent swan song of African art, never to be seen again. This is not to say that contemporary African art is not as good; it simply is not the same, because the spirit and the purpose of creation has changed. As an artist, Laye is not and cannot be like his father; a new world has slipped between them. But he cannot forget that he has witnessed the past, and that he is also a part of this past. Laye came to understand African art in a place in which it did not belong, in Paris, in the Musée de l'homme, and he realized that it did not belong there because in the museum it had lost its meaning, its intent, and therefore its raison d'être. It was in his father's workshop that it was truly art, as his ancestors had understood it, and their particular conception of art is no more, even though African art goes on. Thus, it is as an artist that Laye is truly his father's heir. It is in this capacity that he too is the chosen one, the vehicle for the guiding spirit of the race. It is he who, through the magical rhythm of the written word, has captured the intangible spirit of the Malinké and allowed its values to enlighten the future; it is the imagery of the ancient world that constitutes the main infrastructure of his symbolic and metaphorical language.

The Mother's World

The events witnessed in the father's workshop are so striking that it is easy to understand why they are the first to surface as Laye attempts to analyze and to give order to his childhood memories. Yet the book begins with a long dedicatory poem to his mother, which gives a good insight into the depth of his feelings for her and the magnitude of her influence on his poetic vision. The poem's first line, "Black woman, African woman, O thou my mother, I think of thee," clearly emphasizes that, for the author, the image of the mother is a metaphor of black womanhood, a magnified projection of eternal motherhood which is a further symbol of the motherland and of Africa. The French critic Gaston Bachelard believes that "filial love is the first active principle to induce image projection, it is the projecting force of the imagination, the inexhaustible energy which takes possession of all images in order to place them in the most secure human perspective: the maternal perspective."[28] The maternal image projected as a symbol for the motherland is not unusual in African letters, but Laye's portrayal of his mother is so powerfully drawn that she also becomes the archetype of African motherhood, while still retaining the warmth and vulnerability of a real character.

Her presence pervades the entire book. Her authority is felt by everyone in the household and her insistence that tradition be observed in all its daily manifestations is duly obeyed. Her influence extends beyond the home, and she is greatly respected by her friends and neighbors. Laye gives an explanation for his mother's respected position—"This had to do, I believe, with my mother's very character, which was impressive; it pertained also to the powers she possessed"[29]—and then proceeds to tell us that his mother had supernatural powers and could do prodigious things. Again, he insists on the fact that although he cannot explain the wonders he has seen, and his scientific and modern education denies their existence, he knows he has seen them. "In our country there are mysteries without number, and my mother was familiar with all of them. Like her husband, she belongs to the smith's clan and is singled out as one who has 'inherited the spirit of her caste.' "[30] She, too, is usually warned in dreams of possible dangers or future events, and for this reason is never awakened for fear of interrupting an important message. But, unlike the father, she is a witch, albeit a benevolent one; she can prevent evil but cannot inflict it, which explains why the people respect her but do not fear her. Her powers stem from her birth, which followed that of twin brothers: for the Malinké, as for many other peoples, twins are endowed with special powers and the child directly following is even more powerful. Her totem, inherited from her father, is the crocodile. Consequently, she does not fear the voracious reptiles and is the only one in the community to draw water when the river rises and crocodiles are everywhere. This maternal immunity, readily accepted by all as a natural thing, impresses the child and fascinates the adolescent, removed in time, space, and culture from his mother's archaic world.

The mother's powers are different from the father's in that they manifest themselves often, and in the context of everyday life. They are not linked to any craft or artistic production; they do not transform supernatural forces but only utilize them as need arises, such as in curing a sick animal, preventing a possible crisis, or drawing water in dangerous times. This is not to suggest that the author is less impressed by his mother's powers than by those of his father, but rather that he sees them in a different light, and this is reflected in his writing. The father's world is present in the author's aesthetic vision and symbolic bestiary; the mother's influence is found in Laye's poetic vision of Africa and is the basis of his metaphorical language, and, in particular, his water imagery.

Because of her totem, the mother is closely associated with the Niger, the enormous river which dominates the life of the people living on its banks. Kouroussa, Laye's home town, and Tindican, his mother's village, are both on the Niger, and their memory remains in the author's psyche. Water images are abundant in his writings, particularly in his second book, *Le Regard du roi,* to which we shall return. This aquatic imagery, most likely shaped by the mere presence of the Niger, is also a reflection of the mother's totemic immunity, which in fact, extends to the whole family: "this totem allowed all Damans to draw water from the Niger with impunity,"[31] says the author, thus extending the totemic privilege to the "waters of the Niger" and thereby considerably enlarging their protection and making them safe, reassuring, and maternal. Although the author is not a Daman but a Camara, and his own totem is unknown to him, his imaginary world is dominated by aquatic metaphors which are always positive. Water is almost always beneficial in Laye's fiction, and even if it is sometimes threatening and frightening, it never goes beyond the menacing stage and the threat is never materialized. It is evident that maternal immunity is present and has been transferred by the son to his fictional characters and aquatic fantasy.

As mentioned earlier, the mother's image is particularly in evidence as a metaphor for Africa. What makes the memory of the mother stand out is that, unlike the father, she is not only remembered for the supernatural powers she possesses but is also associated with country life, the earth, the beauty of the fields, and the simple dignity of village life. She comes from Tindican, a small village near Kouroussa, and each year in the dry season the boy goes to visit his grandmother and all his mother's family. An entire chapter is dedicated to his annual visit, and his stays in the country stand out for him as ideal moments lived in a perfect place. "In December, all is in bloom and everything smells good; everything is young; Spring seems to unite herself to Summer, and the country, which for months had been swollen with rain and weighed down with dark clouds, takes an overwhelming revenge and bursts out everywhere."[32] This lyrical description of the lovely season and the unlimited joy it procures—the beauty of nature and the rhythmical pulsation of life renewed—is not the vision of a child, but that of a reminiscing adult.

The beauty of the natural environment is harmoniously balanced by the strong sense of community which exists among the village dwellers. The scene of the rice harvest, in which the reapers all work and sing together in harmony, has been interpreted by the critics Edwards and Ramchand as laden with "a disguised polemical intention

. . . to contrast the mechanized and sterile civilization of Europe"[33] with the idyllic rural culture of Africa. Such an interpretation, forced upon the text to prove that Laye harbored some anti-European and therefore anticolonialist feelings, scarcely does justice to the book. It is not a polemical work angrily condemning the mechanical age; Laye was after all studying engineering when he wrote it. It is a book of love.

The exhilarating emotions of the past surge up and burst from the author's memory as he writes about his childhood. His visits to the country, recalled years later and in a foreign country, take on the emotional intensity of a paradise lost, a paradise full of gaiety, song, warmth, ancient rituals, and all the simple pleasures of rustic life, suspended in time and experienced in the same way for generations, a life he will never see again but will always remember. This nostalgic feeling is tied to his mother's people, who have been part of the land for so long, and to his mother, who belonged to this wonderful world. The author associates his mother with the goodness and happiness of village life, and the chapter describing his wonderful country experiences is followed immediately by one in which he describes his life in his mother's hut, and paints a loving portrait of her.

Most African children are close to their mothers, and one of the main factors contributing to this closeness is polygamy. In a polygamous marriage, the father must share his affection with many people, namely his wives and their children, but the wives care primarily for their own children and consequently a child shares his mother only with his siblings. Laye lived in his mother's hut until his circumcision, which took place fairly late. Despite Eustace Palmer's suggestion that Laye's happy childhood could not possibly have been so, because his mother was too stern, she was the most constant influence on his youth.[34] The love that existed between them is always in evidence in his work. After circumcision, when the child becomes a man, the author remembers how saddened he felt when he understood that being a man meant the first break with his mother, the first unbreachable distance between them: "From now on, there was this distance between my mother and me: manhood."[35] The gap widens even more when he leaves for school, first in Conakry and then in France.

Unlike the father, the mother will always be opposed to the child's departure and will never consider his French education as an advantage but rather as a loss and a betrayal. She knows that school will make him a stranger, a man from a different world, and the distance between her and her son will be much more than a generation, but that of a whole culture. For the author, who was to understand and feel his mother's sorrow deeply, the pain of separation turns in time into nostalgia, regret for the warmth of his mother's presence, the happiness of childhood, the longing for his native land, for Africa. The maternal image that Laye carries with him, and which is so overwhelmingly present in his work, was obviously sustained by the most loving and happy of memories, and it explains why his vision of Africa, particularly of its past, is so idealized and cherished.

L'Enfant noir is clearly the cornerstone of Laye's work, insofar as it is the main source of his inspiration; an inspiration drawn, as we shall see, from the now lost world of his parents.

Chapter Three
Dramouss

Introduction

When asked by a journalist to sum up *Dramouss (A Dream of Africa)*, Camara Laye declared, "It is the intellectual adventure of a Malinké tempted by Surrealism."[1] In this novel, the main characters are the same as in *L'Enfant noir,* but the protagonist is now called Fatoman and his sweetheart, Mimi. The story is told in the first person and relates the homecoming of Fatoman after six difficult years as a student in Paris, his marriage to Mimi, the realization that the Guinean political regime is becoming more repressive, and his subsequent return to France. In the short last chapter, Fatoman returns home once more to see his aging father and to witness the further deterioration of the political situation; he observes that nothing is left but the hope of overthrowing the government. Unlike *L'Enfant noir, Dramouss* is not an idyllic rendition of the past, but rather a bitter political statement on the moral frailty of revolutionaries and an attack on the regime of Sekou Touré. Laye left Guinea in 1965 and the book was published in Paris a year later: it was of course banned in Guinea.

Both an intellectual adventure and a political pamphlet, *Dramouss* is artistically inferior to *L'Enfant noir,* and the charm, spontaneity, and poetic tone of the first book are absent. The autobiographical element seems to be merely a pretext for the political message, and the characters are like extras in a play; we know who they are, but we learn very little about them, and they are far less interesting than their situation. However, Africa remains the theme, and the book is dedicated to the author's generation, the first generation of African writers, to encourage them to work for the restoration of authentic African values in which they must find the truth of the future.

The critical reception of *Dramouss* was mixed but uneventful. No great praise or violent controversy came forth at its publication. *L'Enfant noir* was now a grown man and what he had to say was strictly for the grim world of adulthood. Charles Larson has very aptly remarked that ". . . the most striking element, that immediately jolts the reader, is the harshness of the book when it is compared to Laye's first work." He goes on to say that *Dramouss* is "one of the most scathing commentaries on African political institutions written by a Francophone writer."[2] Similarly, Robert Pageard, in a rather laudatory article, points out that "*Dramouss* brings us some of the earliest literary testimony on the conflict which opposes the traditional African spirit to authoritarian collectivism."[3]

It is truly noteworthy that Laye, who had been labeled by some of his earlier critics as a reactionary at worst and a dreamer at best, is one of the first to announce that the dream of independence is slowly turning into a nightmare. This denunciation of the situation in Guinea is proof of Laye's integrity as a man and as an artist, for nobody wanted to hear that Guinea, which had been the first to opt for independence, was turning into a repressive regime. Sekou Touré's "non" to De Gaulle's "French Community" was still echoing as the defiant cry of a people bent on deciding its own destiny. Although no one protested the truth of Laye's testimony, it was viewed by some as an exaggeration or a misunderstanding of the problem, stemming from the author's political conservatism. The Nigerian novelist Chinua Achebe, for example, who admired Laye's first two books, felt that *Dramouss* ". . . is an embarrassing failure, not only because [Laye] evades the issues. I think that he is a conservative, and he doesn't like the change, the change which is coming with independence. It is a very curious situation for an African to be in, but it is true. He doesn't really like this change, and he can't handle it."[4] This statement, made in 1975 when a plethora of accounts of all kinds had come out of Guinea attesting to the veracity of Laye's accusation, stands as a disconcerting lack of judgment on Achebe's part, to say the least.

In the context of African letters, both francophone and anglophone, *Dramouss* leads the way to many subsequent postindependence novels which have as their common theme political disenchantment with the newly independent regimes. In Cameroon, Daniel Ewandé presented a devastating satire of his government in a novel entitled *Vive le Président! la fête africaine* in 1968, followed a few years later by Mongo Beti's *Perpetue* and *Remember Ruben* in 1974. In Senegal, Ousmane Sembene denounced social and political corruption with *Le Mandat* in 1965 and *Xala* in 1973. In Nigeria, Wole Soyinka published *The Interpreters* in 1965, which is followed by Chinua Achebe's *A Man of the People,* and in 1968 the Ghanaian Ayi Kwei Armah expressed his bitterness toward Nkrumah's regime in *The Beautiful Ones Are Not Yet Born*. These titles are simply a partial and early illustration of what has today become African letters' most important theme.

In contrast to their treatment of Laye's former works, critics generally did not question the subject matter of *Dramouss,* but rather its form and style. Most felt that as a work of art the book was a failure. With *L'Enfant noir,* the time lapse and physical distance allowed the author to treat his subject with a certain detachment, essential to the polishing of the form and vital to that illusory truth which is art. In *Dramouss,* on the contrary, the subject matter, at least on the political level, is too recent and too sensitive. Laye wrote the book while still in Guinea and supposedly finished it as early as 1963. The author is too close to his subject, and at times the desire to speak out seems to overcome and cripple the art of storytelling. As in *L'Enfant noir,* Laye composed *Dramouss* to ease his spirit and unburden his soul, although the burden was of a very different nature. In an interview with Jacqueline Lenier, he explained that writing the book was a liberation, a catharsis, and when the book came out he regained his peace of mind: "I was no longer thinking of it. I had forgotten my obsession. It is like going to a doctor, I was cured."[5] He goes on to say that what he really had to tell was how bad Sekou Touré's regime had become, and how serious the consequences of such a government were for the country and the people.

Therefore, unlike *L'Enfant noir,* in *Dramouss* the autobiographical element is secondary in intent and in appeal, as is often the case in a sequel. Consequently, the main character, Fatoman, seems a tourist in his own life, always visiting, never really fitting in anywhere, but not wanting to, either. His years as a student in Paris lead him to reflect on the materialism of Western culture, and the trip home makes him aware of the numerous changes that have taken place— not all of them bad—and of the rapidly deteriorating political situation. The dialogues are often very stiff or trite, despite the close relationship which exists between the characters and the importance of the subject discussed. As Robert Pageard has pointed out, Laye has the quality of his faults and his integrity, intelligence, and moral sense are responsible for some of the very pertinent remarks on art, culture, and politics to be found in the book. They belong, however, to the essay, not to the fictional mode. A good example is the long dissertation that Fatoman's father delivers on traditional art. It is an interesting vision of African art, which is, however, quite unbelievable and unacceptable, coming from a supposedly traditional crafts-man. In *Dramouss,* Laye fails many times to transpose reality so as to make it ring true for the reader. The critic James Olney summarizes accurately the failures of the book: "*A Dream of Africa* proves that no amount of talk about how things are different can replace the creative effort or reenacting the way they were in the past or the way they are in memory."[6]

Flawed as it may be, the book does have redeeming values and, for our purpose, the interest of the novel lies in its imagery, rooted as it is in the past, and in its structure, insofar as this differs from the Western norm. This does not mean that the structure of the book is revolutionary or attempts to transform the novel as we know it; in-deed the author readily acknowledges Western influences such as that of the Surrealists and of the techniques of Kafka. Rather, it is the rhythm and the animating spirit of the novel that make it non-Western. The repetitive period which characterizes Laye's prose in his two previous works is not so evident here, but the structural pattern of the book generally reflects African aesthetics and its particular view of reality and time.

The author interrupts his narrative twice, for example, once to lis-ten to a griot's tale and again to narrate for an entire chapter the pro-tagonist's dream. Although the two digressions are related to the story, their connection with it is not immediately clear to the West-ern reader. It is evident that the chronological events of the plot rep-resent only one part of reality, and the digression another. Laye par-tially explains his aesthetics through the character of the father. As in *L'Enfant noir,* one chapter of the book is set in the father's work-shop, but this time he is sculpting a wooden object for European tourists, and while working he expresses his views on art past and present:

Our elders, he answered, did not copy reality; they transposed it to such an extent that something abstract inserted itself into the image of reality that they produced. However, it is not a systematic abstraction, but rather an abstraction which appears as a means of expression stretched to the limit, unsure of its limit. But our elders did not usually put as much calculation into their transposition of reality; they used to let their heart speak freely; and thus their transpositions led them to a distortion which first underlines and accentuates the expression and the spirituality, and which consequently then provokes other distortions, but this time purely for plastic reasons to offset the first ones and to realize them.[7]

Furthermore, the father adds, art is now totally devoid of spirituality and is consequently nothing more than an ornament, or at best an aesthetic pleasure.

As an African artist expressing himself in a Western medium, Laye is of course wearing two hats, but it is evident that his writings are infused with an ancient spirituality: for him, the poet is the messenger of God. As the father had stretched and worked the gold thread to materialize his idea of beauty, Laye stretches and works his story line to formulate his political and social ideals.

The Griot's Tale

The Griot's Tale occupies almost all the third chapter, which is situated in Kouroussa, where the protagonist has returned for the first time in six years. The visit also provides an opportunity for Fatoman to introduce his bride to his parents. It is at the young woman's request that the Griot tells a story of the wealthy, pious, and jealous Imam Moussa, who asks God to give him a second wife, just like the first one: beautiful, fertile, and faithful. The answer to his prayer is divine laughter, followed by the remark that his wife might be beautiful and fertile, but that faithful she is not. The incredulous Imam asks for proof and God provides it. Despite his jealous vigilance the Imam has been a cuckold for ten years. The wife's lover is an ugly, poor, filthy, and crude shepherd who is the father of two of the Imam's three children. Confronted with the facts, the Imam's faith in God is strengthened but his distrust of women increases. He repudiates his wife, marries again, and fathers a daughter. To save the child from her morally weak feminine nature, he raises her as a boy. Notwithstanding her father's best efforts, the girl blooms into a very pretty young woman whose beauty is second only to her feminine intuition and shrewdness. Although totally inexperienced, she succeeds in deceiving the king and the entire court in order to save her father from being caught in the queen's bedroom, thus proving that woman's nature is not to be denied.

Like most tales, the Griot's Tale offers different levels of understanding and various themes. Women are uncontrollable and order might be better kept if husbands loved their wives more and watched them less. On a more philosophical and less obvious level, there is the glorification of God and his divine wisdom. His spiritual presence dominates the tale, teaching the Imam and guiding him through his domestic ordeal, and in addition to the humor and irony usually present in a cuckold story, the religious overtones are very strong. The Imam, often portrayed in contemporary African literature as greedy, hypocritical, and ridiculous, is a rather sympathetic character and a genuinely religious man. Of all the tales that exist in African folklore, it is important to notice Laye's choice. He had used the story before, as a radio play for the Guinea National Radio, thereby revealing his interest in such themes.[8] Although it appears to be a digression arresting the narrative flow, it is in fact a bridge between the autobiographical and the personal dimensions of the plot, and the political and moral message yet to come. The conjugal problems of the Imam provide a practical lesson for Fatoman and his bride, as well as a general statement on human frailty.

The theme of jealousy runs through the entire novel, but interestingly enough it is only the female characters who are jealous. Mimi is jealous of Fatoman's life in Paris, suspecting that he has been unfaithful, and before consenting to their marriage she insists on a promise of monogamy from him. Later, Fatoman is dramatically awakened from his long dream because his hut is on fire. Family and neighbors are at a loss to explain the cause of the blaze. But everything becomes clear when the father realizes that Fatoman and Mimi have slept in the same bed. Fatoman's dream was no accident, but induced by the father with the help of a little white ball which he gave to his son, with orders to put it under his pillow and to ask God to enlighten him as to the future of Guinea. The father already knows the future through his communication with the little black snake, but the son, who has no direct contact with the spirit of the land, must rely on his father's powers. However, the father forgets to tell him that, in his dream, the future will be revealed by a woman, a fantastic symbolic figure, and in order for her to appear he must sleep alone. Irritated by what seems a disdain of the rules, and jealous of Mimi, she has set his hut on fire. To this revelation the father adds, "Women are always jealous."[9] Although she is a spirit, a vision, her female characteristics are the same as if she were real. This feminine moral flaw not only reflects ancient African misogyny, but by the same token underlines the spiritual strength of the hero. Fatoman is immune to jealous feelings because, as he says, he trusts people; his moral fiber is somewhat stronger than that of the other characters of his age group, thus explaining why he has been chosen to dream the future.

Dramouss

Fatoman's dream begins with the image of a giant standing in front of a dark house surrounded by a wall. The giant picks up the hero by the feet and hurls him high in the air and over the wall, where he floats slowly to the ground. There, he is prisoner in a house which is a terrifying place, where human life has no value and God's existence is denied. The whimsical and cruel decisions of the giant are the only rules. The hero protests, of course, against the tortures and inhumanities he witnesses, and quickly finds himself the next victim. At the moment of execution, he suddenly turns into a hawk and briefly flies away from his tormentor, who in turn becomes a bird, a much larger one, which tries to bring the protagonist back down inside the prison wall. It is then that a large black snake appears in the sky, telling Fatoman to hold on to it because it has come to save him. Fatoman grabs it by the neck, and the snake rises swiftly like a rocket, escaping the gunshots coming from the ground. Looking down, the hero first sees smoke, then a fire, and the snake explains that the smoke symbolizes evil and political intrigue, and that the fire means that Fatoman is saved because of his righteousness and his humanitarian spirit. The pair travel through the air for a short while before landing suddenly. It is night and the snake turns into a beautiful woman with magnificent hair down to her ankles. She identifies herself as Dramouss, and then disappears. She will appear and disappear several times during the dream. Fatoman is now near the river Niger, in a village he used to know but now hardly recognizes. The population has diminished and many people have either died or gone away to other lands. It is still the same place but nothing is the same; totally disoriented, the dreamer waits for help at the foot of a giant tree. For several hours nothing happens, but Dramouss finally reappears, and with her the vision of many corpses now surrounding the tree. She orders Fatoman to fetch another dead body, which is to be found down the road. This turns out to be himself, a victim of the "revolution." The ground is then suddenly flooded, and everything, including the hero, is threatened by the deluge. Dramouss returns once again, and her eyes are like two enormous headlights shining on a dual vision of heaven and hell, as two human columns representing happiness and despair march past both sides of a billboard, on which one can read a verse of the Koran, "On this earth, man does nothing for anyone, and nothing against anyone, he does everything for himself or everything against himself."[10] Then everything vanishes, swallowed up by the flood, just as everything has been swallowed by the revolution, as Dramouss says. From the devastating waters she has managed to save a little golden bough, the symbol of leadership, and of the gun, the assegai and the daba,[11] which she will give to the heroic black lion, future savior of the land. As Fatoman takes the golden stick, it turns into a pen. We now come to the last vision of this long dream: the moon suddenly detaches itself from the heavens and comes down to the water, toward the half-drowned hero who then goes into the moon and sits inside. As he looks around, he notices that a rope connects the moon to the sun. Dramouss is next to him as they slowly rise toward the sun, guided by the black lion. When they are above the abyss, the moon becomes Guinea, a happy Guinea led by the heroic and wise black lion.

Laye does not use the dream as the structure of his message in order to disguise and somewhat blunt the content, but rather to strengthen what he has to say. In Malinké culture, dreams are messages from God or from spirits and are taken very seriously. Camara Laye, as a deeply religious man, sees no contradiction between Islam and the ancient animist beliefs which are the pillars of African traditions and values. Like other artists of his generation, Laye views the old animist beliefs not as irrational superstitions but as the key to a specifically African metaphysical order, a source of ancient ideals on which modern Africa should be based in order to contribute fully to the civilization of mankind. Thus, the premonitory dream has been used by the Malinké to warn since the beginning of time, to predict, to advise as to which path to follow, to curb man's folly and to remind him that he is not the master of the universe and that he cannot disturb its perfect order with impunity.

Fatoman's dream is clearly Laye's warning and prediction, and in fact, in 1963 at the Colloquium on African Literature at Fourah Bay College in Freetown, Liberia, the author recited the "Dream of the Black Lion" in lieu of reading a learned paper, saying that he had dreamt it the night before, and that there was no better way to speak of Guinea's soul than to speak of its dreams. As remarked above, *Dramouss* was already finished at the time of the colloquium so the veracity of Laye's remark about dreaming of the black lion can be questioned. It is, of course, of no great importance, and authors, like everyone else, are entitled to a white lie here and there, especially when their safety is threatened by the truth—Laye was still living in

Guinea at the time. It is, however, the differences between Laye's dream and Fatoman's dream which are interesting. In Laye's dream, the entire prison sequence is left out; no mention is made of the giant, the snake, or the hawk; and the word revolution is not pronounced. All the other symbols, such as the flood, the magnificent woman, humanity grouped in two columns, the golden staff, the black lion, and the trip to the moon, are present. So that there would be no misunderstanding, Laye explained the major symbols: ". . . If we know that in our eyes the moon and the sun symbolize progress and success, and the lion strength, we shall understand quite simply that it concerns the end of an old regime and the birth of a new age in the continent of Africa, and in the other continents. And then, on the other side of, or through, that first reality, there is a second and deeper one which exists altogether on another plane, somewhere between man and God. For is not the fine woman, so extraordinarily beautiful, the symbol of justice?"[12] Laye's dream was deliberately vague and could fit any African country three years after independence, when most leaders were, at least publicly, searching for progress, success, justice, and the establishment of a new age. In the old tradition of African storytellers, Laye made it clear that his dream also existed on another plane and contained meanings not always readily accessible. Three years later, when *Dramouss* appeared, it became evident that the key to Laye's dream was to be found in Fatoman's.

In the novel, the political message is clear and can be summed up briefly: the evil giant is of course Sekou Touré, whose revolution is ruining the country, and the only salvation is to overthrow the government, thus opening the way for a new leader and a new regime symbolized by the Black Lion. Laye's political role in Guinea and his negative appraisal of the regime need not be considered at length here, as they do not bear significantly on the subject of this essay, but the allegorical language through which the message is conveyed remains to be analyzed.[13]

Like the tale, the dream is twofold. The first part is a description of the situation and a dialogue between Fatoman and the giant, in which the author exposes not only the physical tortures and barbarous conditions of the prison but also the immorality and corruption of the regime. In contrast, Fatoman stands for freedom, love, social justice, and God, namely Laye's conception of the ideal society, which, like many Utopian societies of the eighteenth century, is based on virtue.

For Laye, however, virtue comes from God, and his views reflect Islamic theology in its most profound belief: total submission and obedience to God, in fact the meaning of the word Islam itself. For the author, the giant's evil doings are a direct consequence of his atheism, and, although not stated directly, of his Marxism. Politically and culturally, Laye is attached to the past and his ideal political system would have been a blend of Western democracy and ancient African political institutions.

In his private correspondence with Mrs. Carducci, which she has kindly let me read, Laye expresses some of his political views. For example, he reproaches Sekou Touré for having successively allied himself with the wrong nations, such as Russia, Cuba, and the United States; these allies have brought with them their financial help and their scientific knowledge, ideologies unsuitable to Guinea. A deeply religious Moslem, Laye was strongly anti-Marxist. At the same time American capitalism did not appeal to him, since he found it excessive and too materialistic. In his mind, France was the best Western ally for Guinea, because of the language and the cultural bonds that already united the two nations.

The second part of the dream begins with Fatoman's miraculous escape, and ends with the hero's awakening. The symbolic language gives a dreamlike quality to the events, and the author mixes Western and African images, thus giving an impression of timelessness. He also introduces a rather extensive bestiary, which seems totally African in inspiration. The first symbolic image is that of the bird; Fatoman turns into a hawk in order to escape his tormentor. This sudden transformation into another form of life is common enough in all fairy tales, and African folklore is no exception. It usually occurs as a means of protection or mystification. Fatoman does not will his transformation, but it does happen when most needed, which implies protection from positive forces or from God. In almost every culture, birds symbolize spiritualization; in ancient Egypt, for example, the hawk was the emblem of the soul. More significantly, however, it must be noted that in Laye's version of the Soundiata epic, the totem of the conqueror's personal griot is the hawk.

Fatoman is obviously speaking for the author, and the griot, who is the historian and storyteller of ancient Africa, is in many ways the precursor of the contemporary African novelist. Through his writings he is the witness and the memory of his times, but, unlike the ancient bard, he owes allegiance to no one. His conscience is his mentor. This flight from danger can also be seen as an aspiration toward spiritual values and a desire to reach God, creator and dispenser of all good. The fact that the tormentor also becomes a bird, a huge bird of unstated species, shows that evil forces have power, too, and can transform themselves at will in order to pursue their victims. However, the huge bird does not surge upward to catch Fatoman in the air, but rather tries to bring him back down to the ground, the symbol of the materialistic realm instituted by the Giant. It is also possible that Laye uses the hawk as an uplifting symbol, in reference to a gesture of Sekou Touré:

Sekou Touré in an immense meeting of the people on the occasion of Guinea's independence, in front of the crowd assembled in the evening, had a captive hawk released, which whirled a bit at first, drunk with its recovered liberty, before flying off in the vast sky, charged with all the promises of the world. [14]

In Fatoman's dream, however, it is not the hawk which bears the promises of the future but the Black Lion. This symbolic displacement is further reinforced at the end of the novel, when Fatoman's father, through the sheer power of prayer, recalls a hawk which has just flown away with a chick and forces it to bring back its intended victim. The father then explains that faith in God is power, and that prayers are stronger than political speeches; the hawk is a thief, but with God's help it can be made to bring back what it has taken.

The Black Lion will fulfill the broken promises of the Giant. This message is first announced by the large black snake, which of course recalls the father's totem. Although in Fatoman's vision the snake is now as powerful and as fast as a rocket, it is simply an updated version of the same spirit. Its presence brings protection and wisdom, and is the sign that Fatoman has been chosen to preserve the ancestral values and to accomplish God's will. The hero has been condemned by the Giant for his righteousness, and saved by the snake for the same reason. It can safely be assumed that Laye saw himself as his father's spiritual heir, and perhaps as a spiritual leader for his country. But if the spirit of the race continues to manifest itself in the next generation, it also takes on a totally new form: that of a beautiful woman called Dramouss, whose name is in fact the original French title of the book.

Dramouss, like the other allegorical beings of the dream, is giant size, to symbolize the strength of justice struggling with the forces of evil. More significant, however, is the femininity of the new symbolic image. Dramouss is a mysterious woman "with fine features, light skin, beautiful without compare, with extraordinarily long hair covering her shoulders and her back and falling to her ankles."[15] As the new manifestation of the black snake, she bridges the gap between Africa's past and present, between the dark child and his parents. Like them, she embodies the ancestral values and insists that they must be followed. She teaches Fatoman all he must know, saves him from disasters, and shows him the way to a better future, whose hope she bears within her.

In thus symbolizing Africa's future, Laye shares a common vision with his contemporaries; the image of woman is universally positive in the francophone African novel, regardless of the philosophical and political views of the writer. Although their visions of an ideal society differ greatly, their image of the future always includes the African woman, although Laye gives the common symbol a new force by making Dramouss a mixture of black and white beauty. Great emphasis is placed on the length of her hair, which, in the interpretation of symbols, means spiritualized energy, and she breathes new energy into the future. She knows and believes in the ancient moral values, but she is also turned toward the future and the West; in fact, at one point, already mentioned, the author describes her eyes as giant headlights shedding a merciless light on humanity. She shows the "revolution" to be a flood destroying everything, but as in the biblical flood, the truly good will survive, and to the ancient symbols of leadership that she has saved from destruction, she adds the pen, an unmistakable reference to the author and to that generation of writers to whom he had dedicated the book. The written word is a new power in Africa, and writers must be permitted to use the pen to serve and lead their nations. It is of interest to note that, to illustrate the destructiveness of the revolution, Laye uses the mythical image of the flood. It is noteworthy because the myths of the flood which exist in most cultures are rarely found in Africa, and only once in the author's otherwise abundant water imagery.[16] It can thus be assumed that the image was most likely inspired, at least in part, by the biblical myth with which Laye was familiar. There is, however, considerable manipulation of the myth on the author's part, and he uses it mostly on the literary level: for example, the time is no longer biblical but historical. The flood, although occurring in a dream, represents a specific event happening in a definite country at a determined time: contemporary Guinea. The destruction is also narrowly defined, as it involves only one African country and not all of humanity. Unlike the biblical flood, the scourge is not divine here for it is man who causes the flood, and the waters are a metaphor for the revolution. It is furthermore clear that the waters are telluric in origin, not celestial. They are not spiritual waters, they are not divine punishment, but the inevitable consequences of evil. They occur unexpectedly, and the hero is taken by surprise: "as I was looking down, I understood with renewed fear that the ground had been suddenly but very evidently flooded."[17]

The inundation is caused by "two immense torrents" which are referred to later as oceans. Fatoman, pursued by the rising waters, takes shelter in a giant tree, soon to be engulfed by the menacing tide. It is the moon which comes down from the heavens to save the hero, thus acting like the biblical Ark, and as we have seen, Fatoman goes into the moon and is saved.

The lunar image, coupled with that of the waters, is undeniably feminine in origin, and can be interpreted in light of the maternal influence on Laye. The unrealized threat of the dangerous waters recalls the totemic immunity of the mother and in symbolic language, the moon is always feminine "and equated with the symbolism of the number two."[18] The fact that the moon is a metaphor for Guinea strengthens the femininity of the image, for in French, Guinea is also feminine. Clearly, the metaphorical language of Fatoman's dream is predominantly female and decisively positive. Dramouss's hybrid nature represents Laye's political and cultural concept for the future of Guinea and of Africa, for he considered himself a cultural mulatto. In this, he follows Senghor's theory of "the Civilization of the Universal," which posits that black values awakened by the Négritude movement will bring African culture into the world stream, to intermingle and to work toward the accomplishment of universal civilization.

The new hope embodied by Dramouss will be fulfilled by the "heroic and wise Black Lion," a symbolic figure inspired by Soundiata, the thirteenth-century conqueror and creator of the Empire of Mali. One of Soundiata's totems is the lion, and it is also the totem of the Keïta, the royal family of Mali. The mythical Black Lion is linked to the sun, which, in the dream, symbolizes light and progress. In Africa, the mythology of the sun and the moon is not abundant, but in mythological stories they often appear together, representing the opposite but complementary forces of life: namely, male and female. Here again, Laye relies on tradition to inspire him with a metaphor that illustrates and illuminates the future. As both historical figure and legendary hero, Soundiata represents a political ideal of justice, probity, strength, magnanimity, and obedience to the will of God. For Laye, the Black Lion, whoever he may be, is the heir of Soundiata and will guide Guinea out of the abyss in which she is now foundering, toward "the sun, source of light and progress."[19]

Although the book does not work well as a novel for the reasons we have stated, Laye's vision is obviously that of a poet for whom dream and reality are one and the same. Fatoman's dream, in which the author's main purpose is to convey a political message, provides clear insight into Laye's creative process, and into his manner of working and elaborating his theme into its final multi-dimensional shape.

Chapter Four
Le Regard du roi

Introduction

Le Regard du roi (The Radiance of the King),[1] published in 1954, one year after *L'Enfant noir,* is without doubt Camara Laye's best-written work and one of the most interesting of all African novels. It is usually classified as a mystical and philosophical novel, a vein only infrequently exploited in Western African literature, but nevertheless graced with such superior works as *L'Aventure ambiguë* of the Senegalese Ch. H. Kane[2] and *The Voice* of the Nigerian Gabriel Okara.[3] Upon its publication, it was very well received by European critics, with Albert-Marie Schmidt in *Réforme,* the Protestant French weekly, declaring that ". . . we never have read anything so dense nor so deep about the dark continent . . . ."[4] Jean Louis Curtis in *Art* felt that Laye was a "Kafka revised by an African Alain Fournier."[5] The African intelligentsia was less enthusiastic, although the book did not provoke the controversy which surrounded *L'Enfant noir.* Mongo Beti found the book politically suspect but the most serious attack came from the Nigerian playwright Wole Soyinka, who accused Laye of having plagiarized Kafka: ". . . most intelligent readers like their Kafka straight, not geographically transposed. . . . It is truly amazing that foreign critics have contented themselves with merely dropping an occasional 'kafkaesque'—a feeble sop to integrity—since they cannot altogether ignore the more obvious imitativeness of Camara Laye's technique. (I think we can tell when the line of mere 'influence' has been crossed.)"[6] Defending himself in the Algerian weekly *Dimanche-Matin,* the author declared:

. . . Kafka's world is not mine. If, like Kafka and many others, I believe "that there is no other world than the spiritual world," it is because that world is mine since childhood, it is because I have never separated the visible world from the invisible one . . . Contrarily to Kafka and his characters, I have never felt isolated nor abandoned in this spiritual world . . . I belong to that world with all the men of my race.[7]

Many years later in the course of an interview published in the Ivory Coast daily *Fraternité-Matin,* Laye remarked that *Le Regard du roi* had been written not according to Kafka's spirit, but only "his technique, which is, in my view, very close to our African temperament."[8] In the same interview, and to further prove his case, Laye, revealing the influence of his engineering training, explained that style can be compared to the different mechanical techniques used to produce energy; just as the same technique can be used to move very different vehicles, so it is with style.

Although written soon after *L'Enfant noir,* Laye's second work is quite different in intent. It is totally fictitious and presents the allegorical tale of a white man's mystical quest in an archetypal Africa. In a way, it is the opposite of *L'Enfant noir:* instead of an African looking back nostalgically toward his childhood and the sweetness of village life, *Le Regard du roi* tells the story of a European, Clarence, turning away from his past and going into Africa in search of his salvation. The works are also structurally different. *Le Regard du roi* is a novel in the classical sense of the term, following all the conventions of the genre; it is narrated in the third person, although primarily reflecting the hero's point of view, and written in the literary past, the *passé simple.*

According to Roland Barthes, this tense is the cornerstone of the narrative because it belongs to the world of fiction, of the conventions of art. "It supposes a constructed world, elaborated, detached, reduced to significant lines, and not a world thrown about, spread out, offered."[9] Although Barthes's comment is meant rather negatively in the context of contemporary French literature, the *passé simple* suits Laye's intentions perfectly, and in his case cannot be viewed pejoratively. Barthes considers the classical novel and its conventions a tired, bourgeois, nineteenth-century genre which no longer corresponds to contemporary French reality, but it did indeed correspond to Laye's reality, for he was not yet a twentieth-century man; in fact he called himself a medieval man whose world was structured, ordered, and dominated by a divine Creator. Laye used the novel as a convention to deliver a message, to extract the essence of reality. However, his use of the third person, which is also a literary convention, is a somewhat modernized version of it. It it not the third person used in the so-called "classical novel" of the nineteenth century as represented by Balzac in which the narrator-author projects a vision of an established order willed and controlled by man. Rather Laye's narrator belongs to the contemporary vision of Flaubert and Kafka, where the character is not in control of his society, but rather its victim.

In *Le Regard du roi,* the protagonist is totally lost in a society he does not understand, and in the spiritual sense, his salvation depends on the dissolution and elimination of his persona. Furthermore, the third-person narrative, along with the use of the *passé simple,* helps to create a genuine fiction, a truthful lie, so to speak. The story of Clarence takes place in a world which stands by itself, related to reality but detached from it. The Africa of the dark child and of Fatoman can be verified, even visited; that of Clarence is not to be found, and yet it exists.

Structurally, Laye's second book, which is also his first novel, is his best. The whole story unfolds in the dreamlike atmosphere of an absurd world, absurd because its logic is unknown to the protagonist, although it is clear to all the other characters. The stylized decor and the unspecified historical time give the story a timeless element, in keeping with the subject, since "religion in general and mystical quest in particular are as permanent as human existence itself."[10] The novel is divided into three parts, "Adramé," "Aziana," and "The King," corresponding to the successive steps toward the protagonist's ultimate goal, and therefore deliberately decreasing in length as the goal comes within reach. There are no loose ends, and all the incidents and characters of the novel contribute to the successful completion of the hero's quest. As a fictional character, Clarence is a sort of Everyman with universal appeal. The other characters, however, are not developed as such, since their main raison d'être is symbolic. They do nevertheless have a human dimension, which is mostly comical, since they are caricatures of human types taken from African life. This humorous side of their personalities acts as comic relief in an otherwise very serious and deeply religious book. Despite the Western structure, the novel is non-Western in inspiration and totally African in its imagery, and the language is an interesting mixture of poetic prose, colloquial French, and repetitions reproducing Malinké speech rhythm.

The novel opens in Adramé, a city of the north, where we meet Clarence, who has lost all his money gambling and thus has had his belongings confiscated by the white hotel manager. Left with nothing but the shirt on his back, Clarence decides to go to the esplanade, where the whole city is awaiting the arrival of the King, since he sees the King as his last chance and hopes to approach him in order to ask him for a post. The crowd is so dense, however, that Clarence is unable even to come close to the royal entourage, and only sees the King from afar. He is, however, struck by the majesty and the frailty of the young African monarch.

In the crowd, the protagonist befriends a beggar and two mischievous youths bearing very similar names, Noaga and Nagoa. The beggar tells Clarence he will intervene for him with the King, but his intervention does not help; he then advises the hero to go south because the King will most likely go there on his next journey. The beggar offers to be his guide, Clarence accepts, and before starting out, he takes his three companions to the run-down native inn where he is now staying, and treats them to a meal. For payment the innkeeper wants Clarence's jacket, and the latter grudgingly gives it to him. As the protagonist and his three companions are about to leave the city, Clarence is arrested by the police because the innkeeper accuses him of having taken back his jacket. The accused protests his innocence, not knowing that the two boys have, in fact, stolen the jacket. He is then dragged to the court house, which turns out to be a Kafkaesque maze of corridors and rooms where he is quickly judged and pronounced guilty in a kangaroo court of the worst kind. Upon the beggar's advice, he flees before the verdict is pronounced. Lost in the court house maze, he is unexpectedly saved by a bare-breasted dancing girl, who takes him to her home, where the beggar and the two boys are waiting for him; then he discovers that the girl's father is the judge whose tribunal he has just fled, although she herself denies it.

Amazed and confused by what he has just gone through, Clarence follows the beggar and the two boys to the southern village of Aziana. The road to the south crosses a lush, fragrant forest whose odors have an intoxicating and soporific effect on Clarence. In Aziana, thanks to the beggar, he obtains an audience with the Naba, who is the chief of the village and the youth's grandfather. The Naba offers to let Clarence stay in the village to wait for the King, in exchange for some unspecified services. Having accomplished his mission, the beggar soon departs, during the night, with a donkey and a woman. To make his stay comfortable, Clarence is given a hut of his own and a wife, Akissi. He befriends the congenial Samba Baloum, the Naba's eunuch, but does not meet the approval of the Master of Ceremonies, a rather spiteful and self-righteous character who acts as the Naba's watchdog.

For a long time, Clarence cannot comprehend why he is given shelter, food, and a woman, since he is never asked to do anything. Finally he understands what everyone else already knows: the beggar has sold him to the Naba as a stud, and every night a different woman from the Naba's Harem comes to visit him. Drugged by the odor of the flowers that Akissi puts nightly at the head of the bed, he is unable to distinguish between his wife and the others. Although he has felt from the beginning that things were not as simple as they appeared, and has felt secretly ashamed of his unbridled sensuality, it is the sight of all the mulatto children who people the harem that makes him understand the services he has rendered. Upon this discovery, Clarence is disgusted with himself and feels unworthy of the King. Bitter and frustrated, he decides to leave the village to get away from everyone and takes refuge near the river, where he has a nightmare about creatures half-fish and half-woman, with provocative breasts, which he finds at once attractive and repulsive. After the dream, Clarence becomes obsessed with the King's arrival and goes to see Dioki, an old woman, who can read the future; she tells him that the King is on his way to Aziana. When he finally arrives, Clarence has lost hope of being seen and received by him because of his unworthiness. But his humility and good will are his salvation, and the King opens his arms to him and takes him to his bosom "for ever."

The fascination of this novel comes from the multiplicity of its themes and their different levels of interpretation, as well as from the wealth of its imagery. European and African critics have been fascinated and puzzled by Laye's novel, and it has given rise to an extensive body of critical analysis. There are disagreements as to the meaning of the book and the critics can be divided into two main factions: those who emphasize the book's religious-mystical theme, as we do, and those who see it mainly as a Négritude novel with religious overtones.

One of the first critics to insist on the Négritude aspect of the work is Janheinz Jahn, who, contesting J. A. Ramsaran's religious interpretation, maintained that "African thinking" was the main and most important source of the novel. To him, "the whole book can be considered as a lesson in African wisdom."[11] Wole Soyinka, many years after his original denunciation, in a rather positive critique of the book sees the latter as a "paradigm of the deeper African reality, a mysterious and complex paradigm in opposition to the simplistic and the naturalistic, the immediately accessible." However, for Soyinka, "despite the mystical effusion at the end, the aesthetics of the novel are secular. . . ."[12] Other critics have acknowledged the religious theme but see it only as a ploy and interpret Clarence's redemption as the redemption of the white race through the black one, thus proving the vitality and spiritual superiority of African culture. In the same line of thought, J. J. Achiriga defends the thesis that Laye's novel is a revolt against colonialism and white culture. However, he recognizes that his argument is difficult to sustain all through the book, because some of the African values presented are not particularly positive. There is no denying that, on one level, the story can be seen as a satire of the white man in Africa and, by the same token, an affirmation of African values. But it would be wrong to attach too much importance to its literal meaning, for there is no doubt that the author's main thematic preoccupation is with the mystical quest of his protagonist; in fact, deprived of its symbolic meaning, a great deal of the story becomes incomprehensible.

The religious and mystical aspect of *Le Regard du roi* was recognized very early on by a few critics such as Senghor, who felt that the book was truly African because it was a hopeful book and a mystical one. J. A. Ramsaran felt that the allegory of the novel is rooted in Sufi mysticism as well as Christian thought and this hypothesis has been further substantiated and greatly enlarged by Ben Obumselu. It must be noted that it is only in the last ten years or so that critics have paid serious attention to the mystical and allegorical aspect of the book as well as its style, although very few have delved seriously into its symbolism. More than twenty years of independence have allowed a certain critical perspective, and Laye's work is being analyzed more for what it may be saying than criticized for what it does not say. Mongo Beti's perennial attacks have been mostly overlooked by African intellectuals and Laye's political conservatism is less of an issue. In his fine essay on the African novel, Sunday Anozie remarks that, "What Laye claims in his work is not the rehabilitation of African man but of universal man" and "It is not so much what has been done to man that matters but rather what man is doing of himself."[13]

Le Regard du roi has weathered time, controversy, and political changes because Laye's message is timeless and universal. It reads like a triptych, illustrating a man's successful search for salvation. The religious and mystical meaning of the story reflects a harmonious synthesis of Christian and Islamic thought, Sufi mysticism, and Malinké metaphysics, but it is from his father's faith that Laye drew the sincerity of his inspiration.[14] The central metaphor of the book is that of the voyage and of the lone traveler lost in a strange land, illustrating the eternal nature of the spiritual quest. The device of the European in Africa is particularly well chosen since he is the perfect metaphor for man's unjustified arrogance and complacency; and race is not the issue. As David Cook has remarked: "I wonder whether there is another work in which color is made such a definite issue and in which we find ourselves forgetting for long passages that the main figure is of a different color from his fellow characters."[15] Clarence is a symbol for man in general, and Laye treats him with compassion. His satire has no bite and his humor is good natured. Clarence is more naive than malicious and his mistakes stem mostly from ignorance and lack of moral courage; he is not a villain, simply an ordinary man.

Although the book is a mystical allegory, the religious climate is deliberately vague. It is assumed that the hero is a Christian because he is European, but no direct reference is made to his faith; he simply displays a certain sensibility which is usually associated with Judeo-Christian thinking. The religion of the Africans is left ambiguous and appears to be the traditional animist faith, and this noncommittal attitude toward a particular creed emphasizes the universality of the theme. The book tells of the search for God, and God has no denomination. Furthermore, the sympathetic portrayal of the hero betrays Laye's religious humanism: he believes in the ability of man to better himself and the world, and he has faith in the infinite power of divine love. On a more secular level, the dilemma of a man abruptly cast out of his cultural context and left to fend for himself in an unknown environment is part of the author's own sensitivity. For example, Clarence's difficulties with the innkeeper are autobiographical, and Laye recalls a similar incident in *Dramouss.* It may indeed be of interest to note that one of his favorite books was Defoe's *Robinson Crusoe;* there is similarity of plot between the novels of Defoe and Laye, but a crucial difference is that in Laye's vision, Friday is an equal. Finally, Africa itself is symbolic in this story, and stands as a metaphor for life with all its ambiguities, difficulties, and unresolved mysteries.

In this allegorical novel, the images and symbolic characters are analyzed not only as a reflection of Laye's imaginary world, but also in that they provide a coherent interpretation of the hero's quest and of his psyche. The analysis is divided into two parts, corresponding to what might be considered the two main phases of the quest: first, an examination of the protagonist's chaotic and often blind experiences as they unfold from the beginning to the nightmarish dream by the river, and second (from the dream to the end), an exploration of the protagonist's moral anguish as he comes to a realization of his debasement, an awareness which leads him to the royal path.

The Quest, Part I

Water Images. Among the numerous metaphors that enrich the novel, the water images are the most constant, thus revealing an aquatic imagination which explains the fluidity of the text. Laye reveals in his work a poetic fidelity to an aquatic universe and the dreams that flow from it. It is a significant universe and the waters, be they from the sea or from the earth, experienced or dreamed about, have different but always positive symbolic meanings. It must be noted that the first part of the quest is illustrated by images from the ocean and the second part from the river. In Bachelard's view,

the material imagination of the water is a particular kind of imagination
. . . and water is also a kind of destiny, not only the vain destiny of fleeting images, the vain destiny of a dream which does not end, but an essential destiny which is a continuous metamorphosis of the substance of the individual being . . . the individual given to water is an individual given to vertigo. He dies each minute, something of his substance is ceaselessly flowing out of him.[16]

Clarence is a being given to vertigo, pursuing an ideal which seems to move away as he gets closer to it. "Everything is fleeing from me, everything is an obstacle to me,"[17] he thinks. It is the sea and its images that first dominate Clarence's psyche and destiny, symbolizing his quest. To reach the African shore, the hero has had to struggle against the reef: "this bar which defended the red earth and which it had been so difficult to cross . . . the waves had carried the small boat twenty times toward the shore and twenty times it had been thrown back to the high sea. Then, at last, the boat had landed."[18] This hostile sea, which had tried to stop him from coming ashore, announces the difficulty and the depth of the quest that Clarence is going to undertake. Africa, like life, is not easily dealt with and knowledge is painfully and slowly acquired. From the beginning of his adventure, Clarence feels carried, drawn toward his destiny.

While in the small boat, he toyed with the idea of throwing himself into the sea but could not bring himself to do so, at least not literally; however, gambling his money away was to Clarence "like throwing himself into the sea." This reckless gesture was actually like a baptism, and was to determine the course of the rest of his life. In his recent study on the sources of the author's inspiration, Ben Obumselu (quoting Martin Ling's study of Islamic mysticism) points out that Sufi symbolism of the sea is abundant, and quotes as an example the prayer of the Andalusian Sufi mystic Muhi'd-Din Ibn'Arabi: "Enter me, O lord, into the deep of the ocean of thine infinite oneness."[19] It is interesting to note, however, that in reality Clarence never enters the water; he remains on the surface throughout the entire novel. The boat is an intermediary between himself and the violent ocean; to cross the surf is like a rite of passage, an initiation into the future moral struggle and the first premonition of success. Violent or not, the sea is a symbol of life, and birth is always dramatic. The maternal water carries and sustains the hero, and the threat it embodies never materializes. Later, during the nightmare, Clarence will be the boat floating on the surface of the water floating ever closer toward his salvation. As the African shore is difficult to approach, so is the King, and his inapproachability is in turn expressed through water images: while Clarence waits on the esplanade among the crowd, he feels "caught in this crowd as in waters suddenly frozen or as in moving quicksand."[20] Later, as he speaks to the beggar, he asks, indicating the sea of raised hands: ". . . is the king always surrounded by such a sea?" The crowd pressing itself between the King and Clarence, like an insurmountable obstacle, is constantly referred to in maritime terms and compared to the dangerous bar defending the coast. As the story progresses and Clarence moves away from the esplanade that the King has just left, he feels dejected and lonely and thinks of the falling night as "a large pool of water" spreading alongside the palace. Finally, the sea imagery reappears during the exhausting trip south, where Clarence, drugged by the odor of the forest, follows the beggar and the two boys like a blind man. The intoxicating odor is described in maritime terms: "This body of perfume, which is like the real sea, already present in the wind and present on the lips, before being discovered by the eyes . . . it is this at first, but afterwards it is a sea in turmoil, deeply agitated, a sea with its currents and its secret rivers. . . ."[21] The metaphor of the troubled sea most likely stands for Clarence's troubled inner self, into which he is retreating, just as the voyage south is "un voyage intérieur" leading to Aziana and self-discovery. Bachelard thinks "the sea first tells tales before giving rise to dreams."[22] In Laye's work, it is evident that the image of the sea recounts and illustrates Clarence's adventures, their difficulty, and the tenacity and courage of the hero.

However, the sea imagery ceases in Aziana; here the protagonist's introspection is conceived in fresh-water terms. In the village, one of Clarence's great pleasures is his morning shower: he has invented a device whereby his wife, Akissi, climbs on a stool and pours fresh water over him. Here again Clarence does not enter the water, but it falls on him like rain. It cleanses him from the horror of the night and washes away the sticky odor of the flowers, giving him new energy. "The water infused the body with a most pleasant energy, but an energy that had no outlet . . . a gratuitous energy but an energy nevertheless."[23] The sensual pleasure provided by the water has an uplifting effect, and the energy it produces is spiritual. It does not materialize into anything tangible but it fuels Clarence's desire for a new life. His longing for purity is renewed daily, thanks to the energy of the water and the clear light of the morning sun, which is like a "promise," the promise of the radiance of the king.

The Odor of the South. Although described in aquatic terms, the demon of the flesh is symbolized by the intoxicating odor which permeates the entire novel. It is not the Christian, sulphurous odor of sin but the pervasive and soporific smell of self-indulgence. Its presence is overwhelming and its soporific effect so strong that Clarence is actually living his life in a semiconscious state.

In the opening crowd scene, what characterizes the natives, for the protagonist at least, is their odor. "From these men tightly packed together under the African sky, rose a woolly, musky smell, the kind of smell one associates with a herd and which puts one into a kind of torpor."[24] While in the northern city of Adramé, Clarence is pursued by the smell of the "herd" as well as the acrid smoky odor of the city, and with the smell comes a dulling of the senses; Clarence witnesses all that occurs on the esplanade as if in a dream. Finally, in Aziana, his nocturnal activities with the wives of the Naba are induced by the intoxicating perfume of Akissi's white flowers acting both as aphrodisiac and soporific and keeping Clarence from fully understanding what he is doing. Clearly, the tenacious sleep-inducing odor symbolizes Clarence's sensuality and the fact that the flesh can mask the true purpose and true reality of human life, namely, the search for and discovery of divine reality. The Sufis believe that their way "serves essentially the function of reminding man of who he really is, which means that man is awakened from this dream which he calls his ordinary life and that his soul is freed from the confines of that illusory prison of the ego, which has its objective counterpart in what is called 'the world' in religious parlance."[25] During the first part of the quest, Clarence's life is lived in an in-between state of awareness, where he is never quite sure of what is going on and never quite in control of his actions. He is obsessed and dominated by the "horror of the South" and its sleep-inducing smell. The horror of it is that it entails at the same time a somnolence of the spirit and an awakening of the senses. Clarence has become a mystery to himself: ". . . who could have said what had happened? Clarence himself did not know. The odor of the forest, without a doubt; it was surely this pervasive odor which is typical of the South, seductive and cruel, lascivious, shameful. But Clarence was breathing it with disgust, he thought about it with disgust . . . he did not wait for the night to come; he feared it. The animal that was in him was perhaps waiting for it; but as for him, he feared it, he abhorred it."[26] The morning comes as a deliverance; the sun and the fresh morning air dissipate the dejection of the night. The antitheses of night and day, dark and light take on here the conventional sense of purity and sin. At night, Clarence burns with "a dark fire" and "feels naked," but during the day he does not even know that he is naked, for he is like the rest of the people of Aziana. In fact, were it not for the color of his skin, he could pass for a native. "I am exactly like them and was it not better that way? Was it not better than being Clarence? and that was why he followed this path, which was the path of the people of Aziana, which was not his own path. But what was his path?"[27] Laye uses the Gidian expression "suivre sa pente." But his hero, contrarily to Gide's, does not know in which direction he should go, but only that the path he is now following does not suit him. As he waits for the morning light to calm his body and dissipate his anguish, he waits for the radiance of the King to take him out of the daze in which he exists. He senses, rather than knows, that he cannot do it alone and that the path of the King is the right one.

The King. The King is strictly an allegorical figure who never takes on the role of a real character and has no human dimension. Although he is mysterious, he is not ambiguous; he is announced as the King of Kings, as God, which in Islamic thinking means he is

unity. He resolves and contains all the contradictions that are reflected in the material reality in which Clarence exists. He appears at
the beginning of the novel, and the awaiting of his second appearance
is the Ariadne thread leading the protagonist out of the maze in
which he has lost himself. The King's outward manifestation is that
of a medieval monarch whose pageantry and magnificence recall that
of the ancient Sudanese Empire. The splendor and power which accompany his presence emphasize the youthfulness and frailty of his
physical appearance, for he is a young adolescent dressed in white
with a gold turban on his head. His arms and legs are weighed down
by extremely heavy gold bracelets, to the point that in order to salute
the crowd, servants must help him to lift his arms. Clarence is moved
by the youth and frailty of the King, which make him appear to be
painfully vulnerable despite his formidable entourage. To the hero's
astonishment, the beggar explains, "he is young and fragile, . . . but
at the same time he is very old and robust . . . If he were not so
heavily weighed down with gold, nothing could keep him among
us."[28] Or, he goes on, it is the gold that chains him to humanity;
but gold can mean something other than gold, can be a symbol for
the purest kind of love, divine love, and it is this love which is keeping the King prisoner on earth. Laye's symbolism of the purest love,
outwardly represented by the purest metal, can be traced both to Sufism and to his father's workshop. Love is the main theme of Sufi mys-
tics, who believe that "man's whole life is dominated by two realities:
'Thou' and 'I': the lover and the beloved, God and man, . . . love is
the mood of the Sufi, gnosis his aim, ecstasy his supreme experience."[29] After the beggar's comment, Clarence thinks, "Yes, it
seemed that one could really love this frail adolescent, one could
really love him despite the darkness of his complexion . . . But why
'in spite of the darkness of his complexion'? What did complexion
have to do with love?"[30] Nothing, obviously; the Koran teaches that
"superiority in this universal world . . . does not depend on family,
wealth, rank, title, creed or color, but on virtue, love and moral
integrity."[31]

By opening his heart to the King, Clarence has taken the first step
toward his far-reaching goal; or, to use Sufi language, he has taken
the first step upon the spiritual "Path." Concerning gold as a metaphor for divine love, it is a symbolic image which can be found in
many Sufi poets, albeit with differing symbolic meanings; it most
likely originates in the old alchemist belief in the purity of gold,

symbol of perfect union and of immortality. Gold, like love, is associated with fire, the fire of the Forge, the spiritual purity in which the smelting of the ore must be accomplished, and we have seen that this transmutation is part of Laye's psyche. Gold is also associated with the ancient Mali empire, whose emperors were famous for their wealth and in particular for their prodigality with gold. Furthermore, Clarence is intrigued by the King's features, which are not remarkable in any way except for the enigmatic and faint smile; it reminds him of that of an idol and makes the hero uneasy since he does not understand its meaning, or rather is afraid to understand it, as it seems to know what he is looking for: "[the smile was] without a doubt the reflection of an inner life, but what kind of life? Perhaps of that life which is beyond death . . . is it that life that I came to find? Clarence asked himself. Maybe it is, yes."[32] If it is, it seems so unreachable, so far away, that he refuses to pursue the thought. Before disappearing into his palace, the King will be seen on an elevated platform which gives the impression that he is suspended in mid-air, and then, instead of saluting the crowd as he did the first time, he salutes the sky and seems to vanish into it. The palace then becomes vague and distant, and Clarence wonders if the entire event were not just an illusion.

However, the first coming of the King has been dramatized for the hero by a dreadful and incomprehensible incident. Upon looking at the walls of the palace, Clarence had noticed that they were heavily decorated with frescoes representing ritualistic human sacrifice. He had asked the youths for an explanation and as usual got a contradictory answer, but the one that he has accepted, although with difficulty, is that the King sacrifices his most faithful vassals because only their blood is worth shedding; the bad vassals are simply ignored by the King, which is a terrible punishment. Upon this explanation of the frescoes, Clarence hears horrible cries, as if people were being slain and were crying out in agonizing anguish. To Clarence's horror, the frescoes are being reenacted. The spiritual significance of the incident, which is not perceived by the protagonist, has Christian as well as Islamic overtones and seems to posit that the cruelest punishment is to be denied the right to see God, which is the true meaning of Hell, and that to attain divine knowledge man must die to the world, which only the best can do. But, in the end, it is of no consequence that the King seems cruel, distant, and unattainable; Clarence puts all his hope in him and lives for the next encounter with the thought that next time the King might lay his eyes on him and give him "a long look, a long meaningful look, and all would be said, absolutely all."[33]

The Beggar. The beggar is the first character whom Clarence encounters. The beggar is a common figure in African society, since charity is mandated by the Islamic faith. However, in Laye's story, he is an ambiguous character who appears to be the opposite of what he should be. He is arrogant, all-knowing, and influential. He is certainly far more than a simple beggar; he is a teacher, not only for Clarence but for the young boys, with whom he is strict and impatient. He seems to have supernatural powers, in that he can read the protagonist's mind. In many ways, he exhibits all the negative characteristics of the African Marabout, and yet at the figurative level he seems to take on the role of the spiritual master as found in initiation texts, where beggars are often all-knowing guides to be followed and listened to. Moreover, he also brings to mind the spiritual Sufi master: "The Sufi master is the representative of the esoteric function of the Prophet of Islam and by the same token he is the theophany of Divine mercy, which lends itself to those willing to turn to it."[34] As a rule, the spiritual master has already traveled the Path and is therefore able to guide the one who is seeking God through the trappings of the material world, and help him through his spiritual death and rebirth. The beggar, who decidedly does not behave like a saintly master, does guide Clarence toward the South, which is where the King will be. While in Adramé, he helps him through the various pitfalls that an unfamiliar society always presents, and takes him safely through the maze of the African city, in other words the mysteries and difficulties of life. As imperfect as he may be, the beggar is a wise interlocutor for Clarence; his reasoning is philosophical and his advice is sound. He gives him his first lesson in humility by showing him that although he is a beggar, he can communicate with the King and speak in his favor.

Clarence has a difficult time accepting that "a black beggar" could do him such a favor: "It was the word 'favor' that he could not stomach: he was not expecting any favor! He would offer his services to the King for a job, any kind of honorable job and he would be fairly paid in proportion to the service rendered. . . . "[35] But the request is not granted, and the beggar points out that there is no certitude, there are no rights, there is only luck, and Clarence is to try his luck since there is always a chance. The theme of luck is a leitmotiv in the book and is particularly in evidence in the first chapter. The almost obsessive repetition of the word *luck* is not only Laye's way of rendering Malinké speech rhythm, but serves mostly to underline the spiritual meaning of the word and to insist on the semantic complexity that it can take in a religious context. It seems that the author is referring to the Arabic *baraka,* which translates into French as "chance" and into English as "luck." *Baraka* means luck in the sense of that which is willed by God, a blessing caused by divine protection, and by extension divine grace. For the Sufis "divine grace (Baraka) flows too strongly in the arteries of the Universe not to touch occasionally even men who are not following the way."[36] Their vision of God is also that of an all-merciful and loving deity who grants his grace to sincere men of good-will.

The theme of luck serves two purposes in the story; it introduces the concept of divine grace, which is man's hope, and the concept of humility, which is a prerequisite of divine grace. Clarence must lose his white arrogance and understand that all men are equal in the sight of God; all have an equal chance to be touched by divine grace, but they must want it to attain it. This desire for divine grace, which men may obtain through their actions, raises in turn the question of man's freedom and the liberty he has to choose a course of action, which means that he is, at least in part, master of his destiny and instrumental in the realization of his salvation. This understanding is illustrated toward the end of the novel when Clarence, painfully conscious of his degradation, does not dare present himself to the King. It is the eunuch Samba Baloum and the smith Diallo who urge him to seize his chance:

Luck! said Clarence . . . If I had the heart to laugh, I would. Luck . . . Call it whatever you like; but it is the name I give it: perhaps it means nothing; and perhaps it refers to a real thing. How can you tell? All I know is—and I'm absolutely sure of this—that if it exists, it won't be given to you for nothing; you'll get out of it only as much as you are capable of getting out of it. He who asks for nothing must not be surprised if he comes back with empty hands. And in the end, if no one is favored all the time, no one is frustrated all the time . . . luck . . . You see now what I mean. You see what I mean by "luck," and what others call merit.

The beggar used to call it favor.

Give it whatever name you like, said Samba Baloum . . . allow me to call it luck.[37]

The eunuch further explains that luck is not the lot of the clever or the righteous. It is for those who want it, who ask for it, and Clarence must make the effort and seize it. This affirmation of human freedom could be either a Christian or a Mo'tazilite interpretation of the Koran, and in *Dramouss* (in Fatoman's premonitory dream), the koranic verset written on the billboard, affirming that man does everything either for himself or against himself, is used in Islamic theology as an argument for man's free will. Thus it seems that Laye subscribes to this interpretation of the Holy Book, which is a controversial issue in Islamic theology.

The beggar, as Clarence's first guide, fulfills two important functions for the completion of his quest: he starts him on the Path first by stripping him of his ego and second by putting him on the road which leads to the King. He shows him that he does not know anything, and that he is not worth much either, since he has sold him to the Naba for a jackass and an old woman. After the beggar's departure, Clarence is entrusted to the care of the two youths. They remain with the hero until the end, mischievous, but always helpful and caring. The idea of these two characters could have been inspired by Kafka's *The Castle,* as there are evident similarities with the two assistants given to K, particularly in their somewhat comical behavior, but they are symbolically very different. All through the narrative, the two boys act like troublesome guardian angels, and when the King finally arrives, they become part of his entourage and exhort Clarence to present himself to the royal presence. It would appear that the spiritual value of the two characters is koranic in inspiration, as it is stated in the Holy Book, "each man has two guardian angels who write down his good and bad actions."[38] They always contradict each other and take an opposite view on everything, thus perhaps representing the constant battle between good and evil, and, possibly, the outer and inner perception of reality.

Justice as a Metaphor.   The first part of the quest is framed by two incidents where Laye uses the metaphor of the judicial process to underline Clarence's spiritual progress. The first one takes place in Adramé, and involves the hasty and ridiculous trial the protagonist has to go through concerning his jacket. The incident is reminiscent of Kafka's *The Trial* and Clarence, like Joseph K., does not understand what is happening to him and has no chance to defend himself: he feels the odds are against him and his guilt is already decided. But

Laye is not creating a parody of Western or African justice, any more
than Kafka was making a critical analysis of his own society. The
whole situation is burlesque and humorous, and has none of the anguish that marks Kafka's novel; it is a farce at the expense of the protagonist and contributes to his humiliation, stripping him of his arrogance, since he has to run in order to keep his undershorts on
(something he seems to find indispensable to his dignity). The irony
of the situation is reinforced later when Clarence, in contact with the
villagers of Aziana, finds it very comfortable to be naked in public,
and in fact outdoes the natives in all their ways.

Being stripped of one's clothing is like being stripped of one's social importance; it is to be reduced to one's basic worth and nothing
more. The philosophical implications are rather obvious, and represent Clarence's first stumbling steps on the road to humility, in perfect keeping with the beggar's teaching. The second incident occurs
in Aziana and this time Clarence is involved only as a spectator. The
Master of Ceremonies does not like the protagonist and at one point,
out of anger, almost reveals to him what his status is in the village.
Clarence's nocturnal activities were to have been kept from him, and
when the Naba hears of the Master of Ceremonies's indiscretion, he
puts him on trial; the verdict is that he is to be flogged publicly,
specifically on the buttocks, which adds a comical note to the situation; in fact, the whole scene is described in comical terms. Clarence
is present at the beating, like the rest of the village, but unlike the
Africans, he is repulsed by the torture, which he calls barbarous, and
requests that the flogging be cut short. To his surprise, everyone
thinks he is wrong and cruel, even the victim.

By exhibiting compassion to the criminal, Clarence seems to express Christian charity in face of the Naba's pagan justice, which actually is nothing more than another kind of sensibility. It is Diallo,
the blacksmith, who explains to Clarence that his pity for the Master
of Ceremonies was unfounded and unjust; he deserves his punishment, even if his fault has been to tell the truth, for the truth is not
for everyone to know and is not always good to hear. In this, he is
expressing an ancient African value, which has been enforced and respected since time immemorial. Diallo goes on to explain that the
Naba is a just man and justice is neither cruel nor kind, it simply is.
Like the public, he has enjoyed the punishment because it was cruel,
and that is because he is not a man of principle; but the Naba and
the other wise men of the court have enjoyed the punishment because

it was just. It would therefore appear that two different causes could have the same effect. To this, Clarence retorts:

"You mean that the just man and the unjust man are worth the same?"
"I don't know exactly if it is what I meant to say; I do not split hairs: I am only a blacksmith. In fact it should not be what I meant to say; but, in fact, it is pretty much what I wanted to say."
"But this should not be!" said Clarence.
"Well," said Diallo, "just men would be a lot less just, I suppose, if their justice pandered less to their cruelty."[39]

This ironic thrust at the integrity of just men, as well as the comical tone of the flogging scene, point out that the Naba's justice, being human, is a parody of divine justice. In the world, good and bad intentions can have the same effect, but God does not judge on the effect but on the cause.

The character of the blacksmith, always present in Laye's work, introduces the theme of goodwill that will dominate the hero's actions in the second phase of his quest. Diallo is forging an axe for the coming of the King, and when Clarence asks him if the King will come soon, he answers that he does not know, that nobody knows: "each day and each hour we are waiting for him. But we also grow weary waiting for him. And it is when we are the most weary that he appears."[40] When the King arrives, he will give him the axe, which is the most beautiful he has ever made; the thousands of axes he made before were mere practice for this one:

So that this axe will be the sum of all I have learned, it will be like my life and all the effort that I have undertaken in my life . . . but what does the King want with an axe? . . . He will accept it and admire it only to please me . . . There will always be other axes infinitely more beautiful and more deadly than all the ones I will ever be able to make . . . and yet I go on forging . . . Perhaps I am unable to do anything else, perhaps I am like a tree that can bear only one kind of fruit . . . and perhaps, in spite of all my faults, perhaps because I am like that tree and I have no special gift, the King will nevertheless consider my goodwill.[41]

Looking at the fire of the forge and listening to Diallo's wisdom, Clarence turns his thoughts back to his childhood, and the smith of his native village. He is suddenly seized by the regret of his lost innocence, and he blushes because "for a moment, he is the child who blushed at the sight of the man he has become."[42] It is interesting to note that the smith is the only one in the story who has no comical or devious side to his character. He is the only one who is simply himself. His sole symbolic value lies in what he appears to be: a good man. It is also the only time in the novel that Clarence displays any kind of nostalgia over his past. Evidently for Laye, whether he is conscious of it or not, the image of the smith brings on regret for the lost paradise of childhood. The shame that engulfs the protagonist, when he thinks of what he has become, marks the turning point of the novel and of the quest. Burdened by the truth that he can no longer ignore, Clarence leaves the village and seeks refuge near the river.

The Quest, Part II

The Fish-Women. When Clarence leaves the village, turning his back on his shame, the sun is at its zenith and the heat unbearable. Unconsciously, the hero goes toward the large river "as if the coolness of the water had been calling him,"[43] and yet this coolness does not in fact exist in his present context. It is Clarence who imagines it; it is the memory of a coolness experienced in the past which he is now recalling and wishing for. When the river finally appears, it flows "slowly, yellow and sluggish, between muddy banks."[44] This longing for the coolness of fresh and pure waters translates Clarence's thirst for the purity of lost innocence and his wish to be at peace with himself. It seems to him that he will never reach the inner harmony to which he aspires, and yet he feels its intangible presence all around him. His desire for coolness and purity is smothered by the overwhelming odor of the forest, the tenacious and demanding odor of the south which is the materialization of his unbridled sensuality. Prisoner of his carnal desires, Clarence has the impression of existing in a viscous universe where his will and spirituality are dissolving and liquifying, and his sole moral certitude is that he is aware of it and suffering from it. "The odor had thickened considerably; it was falling from the tops of the trees and rising from the earth; and somewhere there was a meeting point, a moving meeting point, which at intervals flowed toward Clarence and was submerging him."[45] Hypnotized and anesthetized by the smell, the heat, and the movement of the water passing before his eyes in an endless flowing rhythm, Clarence falls into a somnolent state, conscious only of being "an abject beast" who cannot forget that he wishes to be an angel. It is in this frame of mind that he has the most terrifying experience of his life. This experience is like a perverse psychodrama in which the protagonist, although unaware of it, watches his subconscious self rising, naked as truth, from the waters of the river. Bachelard thinks that "the imaginary being who comes out of the waters is a reflection which materializes itself little by little, an image before being a living being, a desire before being an image."[46] Thus, Clarence sees, all of a sudden, coming out of the waters "in the middle of the river, near an island situated in the middle of the river, a vague feminine form. A vague figure; because, although the breasts were unmistakably female, the head was more that of a fish than of a woman."[47]

It is not surprising that the image of Clarence's desire should be that of a woman. This vision matches well the activities and sexual obsessions of the hero. Clarence is a European, and the waters of the old continent are peopled with all kinds of naiads and water nymphs, as well as the mermaids who haunt the seas. But the feminine form which comes out of the river is not really a mermaid; the head is not human in shape and it lacks the legendary long hair; it is half-woman and half-fish. The legendary mermaid is a fascinating but fateful creature. She represents one of the more morbid facets of Western eroticism. The fish-woman of Clarence seems to come from another imaginary world pertaining to another culture, that of the author. In an article called "The water and bush spirits of French Guinea," M. de Lestrange explains that

in Siguiri, Kankan or Kouroussa, everyone knows why the "lamentin" which lives in the water of the Niger has a woman's breast. A woman was bathing in the river, she was naked. Her son-in-law arrived on the spot and she only had time to cover herself with a lefa (a wickerwork cover) and to throw herself into the water. Ashamed, she has never dared to come back to earth. The round shape of its tail recalls the roundness of the lefa. The Somoro, fishermen of the Niger, do not kill the "lamentin" whose descendant is a human being.[48]

The aquatic vision which fascinates Clarence is endowed with an "essential" femininity like that of African sculpture, where the aesthetic purpose is not the imitation of reality, but the reproduction of the model's vital forces. Here, the fish-woman, a manifestation of Clarence-Laye's libido, is a nonseductive monster, possessing nevertheless a direct and brutal sexual appeal. It is not eroticism but lust. The erotic wavy hair of the Western mermaid is replaced by a lascivious undulation of the entire body. "The feminine shape was now progressing in an undulating manner through the grasses . . . each time it bent backward, it was showing its breasts, opulent and whitish . . . so that one thought immediately of women, one could not think of anything else but of women."[49] But it is not really of women that Clarence is thinking, but of the sexual pleasure he associates with them. He is confronted for the first time with the shameful vision of his unrestrained sensuality, and within him, shame and desire are in deadlock and struggle.

According to Bachelard, "impurity for the unconscious is always multiple,"[50] and soon the primary vision is tripled and a monstrous trio is undulating on the island, all alike, existing only at the sexual level like the women of the Naba's harem. Clarence is torn between desire and repulsion. Suddenly, the desire to swim toward the island is stronger than his disgust; but dazed by the odor of the South, he falls face down in the mud of the river bank. Half-asphyxiated by the stench that rises from the earth, the protagonist is now at the nadir of his degradation as he wallows in the stinking spongy dirt. He is reduced to a loud groan, to the primeval expression preceding the word, and which distinguishes him from brute matter. It is his groaning which allows him not to sink into oblivion, until he hears voices pronouncing his name and hands lifting him out of the mud. Then, he feels himself gliding, not in the river but on the river. The water, although still flowing, has become telluric and very thick. The heavy substance on which Clarence is being carried is reminiscent of the vital mythical clay of the divine Potter; it begs to be shaped and kneaded into a new form, a new man. The river is like Clarence's soul, a raw material needing to be molded, and spiritualized. The will to transform and transcend basic matter is expressed through colors. "The water, as it had become thicker, had lost its unpleasant yellowish tinge; it now had a silvery tone scattered with shadows of a very fine metallic blue."[51] This beautiful blue is not the reflection of the sky in the water, because the thick foliage of the trees forms a vault above the river, totally masking the sky. The vital elements are all combined in the large telluric river, aquatic in its fluidity, aerated and spiritualized by the color, just like the union of the elemental forces in the smelting of the ore.

Bachelard sees a connection between the softness of mud, which leads to a solidified shape, thus announcing the impact of a will, and the softening of the metal demonstrating the smith's will on solidified matter. But the rigid iron object retains in its essence the memory of its fluidity, because "the dreams which have lived in a soul continue to live in its work."[52] The dreams of the forge are forever present in Laye's images, and the muddy waters of the river are metallic in color and contain the promise of the supreme transmutation, that of Clarence's fusion with the King. It is interesting to note, furthermore, that if the water has a metallic blue tinge, it also has a silvery tint, a milky tint, and thus endows the waters with maternal symbolism, which in this context implies for the protagonist an immunity from the possible danger that exists in the river. The threat is in fact present. As it liberates itself from the mud, the river takes on a menacing aspect, seen in the acceleration of the current, the springing up of many islands, and the sound of an unspecified noise resembling that of huge water falls. The aquatic voyage is now becoming like an obstacle race, and the unfortunate traveler is trying his best to navigate safely. The heavy water has turned into a sticky, oily, thinner mud from which Clarence is struggling in vain to disengage himself. Suddenly, he realizes that the islands are covered with fish-women, standing on their tails, obscenely poking their breasts toward him. Carried away by the current, a prisoner of the sticky river, Clarence now glides on the narrowing waterway lined on both sides with a thick crowd of fish-women. "Clarence saw that the moment would come when not only would he brush against them, but he would bump against them, against their opulent whitish breasts,"[53] and this possibility fills him with disgust.

The multiplicity and shamelessness of the fish-women as a metaphor for the obsessive, relentless, and degrading demands of the flesh has a cathartic effect, as it manifests itself openly for the first time. The desire that Clarence may have felt, at one point, for these monstrous creatures is totally gone; he now feels nothing but disgust; he is free. As the speeding current rushes him toward probable destruction, he is awakened by Samba Baloum and the two boys. He opens his eyes and sees "the sky full of stars and nothing masking the view, no foliage, no vault of any kind."[54] Clarence comes out of the nightmare of his sensuality looking upward toward the sky, toward a brighter future.

It is difficult to determine if Clarence dreamed or daydreamed his experience near the river, but whatever the case may be, it is evidently a premonitory and cathartic experience—cathartic in the modern psychological sense of the term as a means of coming to terms

with one's inner feelings and emotions. Clarence has now a clearer
vision of himself and his weaknesses. The dream has led him to self-
knowledge. As for its premonitory aspect, the dream announces the
eventual success of the quest because no harm comes to the hero. The
importance of premonitory dreams and visions in Malinké culture has
been explained in the preceding chapter, and all that has been said
applies here also. Furthermore, Clarence's dream is significant because
its scheme seems to have been taken from Malinké folklore, particularly the Soundiata epic, which Laye uses or refers to several times.
In 1972, in London, on the occasion of a conference on Manding
studies, Laye gave a paper on "Dreams in Traditional Malinké Society," in which he told the dream that Soundiata's soothsayer had had
before the decisive battle of Kirina. The dream foretells the downfall
of Soundiata's enemy, Soumaoro. The ancient dream, as reported by
Laye, follows exactly the same story line, and has a similar structure
to Clarence's dream, with two exceptions: the fish-women are lion-
men and the protagonist of the dream, Soumaoro, dies. Laye explains
the meaning of the dream, and his explanation sheds light on some
of the symbolism he uses in his own work. He explains that in ancient times, the dream was the privileged medium for the battle of
wills between two enemies. They could meet in spirit and in a
dream, to test their strength, and the outcome of the struggle became reality. As a rule, these nocturnal battles occurred near water,
into which the loser disappeared.

In Clarence's dream, the two enemy forces are the dreamer's sensuality, represented by the fish-women, and his *dyilla*. In Malinké
metaphysics, the whole human being is composed of different prin-
ciples: the *fadi* or "body," which is only the outward form, the *nii,*
which is the spirit or the soul, divine in origin, and the *dyilla,* which
seems to be between matter and spirit or rather a composite of both.
Contrary to the *nii,* the *dyilla* is not divine; it has been created, and
therefore is vulnerable and visible and can be materialized. United
with the *nii,* it constitutes the human personality. It is sometimes
mistaken for the shadow of a person, because it can escape from the
body and exist on its own, as in dreams, where it is the *dyilla,* which
often undergoes the adventures or mishaps experienced by the
dreamer. The Malinké ideal is to control one's *dyilla* during one's lifetime, to detach it from its material component in order to liberate its
spiritual one: it seems that the eternal struggle between matter and
spirit, good and evil, common to all religions, takes place at the level

of the *dyilla*.[55] From all this, it can be inferred that in Clarence's dream, the form that is floating or gliding on the water is the hero's *dyilla,* while his *fadi* or physical shell is left on the shore. This would also explain why it does not go into the water, but remains on the surface. It is evident that Laye's imaginary world and philosophical vision is a harmonious synthesis of Islam, Christian, and Malinké thinking, showing that the common ground in these different thoughts far outweighs the divergences.

Finally, to conclude with Laye's water-images, it is surely the river Niger which is the author's main source of inspiration, although this is partially based on traditional thinking and lore and Sufi mysticism. It is the powerful waters of the great river that flow through Laye's psyche, giving poetic fluidity to his prose and his thinking. It is through the metaphor of the violent and threatening water that the author expresses the struggle between the forces of good and evil, be they political, as in Fatoman's dream, or spiritual, as in Clarence's. In 1976, Laye published a short story called "Prélude et Fin d'un cauchemar," in which he once again uses the scheme of the Soundiata dream as well as the flood scene from Fatoman's dream. The hero of the story is Ramaka, an anagram of Kamara, and the two battling forces are life and death, symbolically portraying the author's fight against the disease that was eventually to kill him in 1980. But in the story, the protagonist wins and once more the menacing waters are powerless against him, protected as he is by the maternal totem.

The Vision.　After the nightmare of the fish-women, Clarence goes back to the village and falls back into his sinful life. But now he is fully aware of what he is doing, "and thus all was in the open, it seemed. But it was only an abject openness; it was pure cynicism."[56] Clarence is not trying to struggle against his weak nature, or to change his life; he has lost all pride in himself and his sole "raison d'être" is the hope that the King will one day be there. To break the monotony of the long wait, and feeling that he has nothing to lose, he decides to go see Dioki, an old soothsayer who lives with snakes in a pit at the edge of the village. He hopes she will tell him if and when the King will arrive in Aziana. He is warned not to go because of the possibly dangerous snakes, and besides, "she never says everything, says Nagoa. She discovers things and she brings them out. But one discovers and sees only what one takes the trouble to look at carefully."[57]

Clarence is determined to keep his eyes open and to see his future.

Upon entering Dioki's hut, he is quickly surrounded by snakes, but she tells him that they are harmless, for those with good intentions. To this, Clarence answers sarcastically with a double entendre, to the effect that she has passed the age of provoking bad intentions in a man. Without warning, a big snake coils itself around Clarence and holds him tightly while staring at him fixedly. Despite his fear, the hero notices the strange beauty of the beast and the cold indifference of its stare. Dioki tells him to keep still and not to ill-treat her with either words or deeds; the snake is about to speak and she will repeat everything it says. The message is that the King is coming, and will arrive one afternoon, although nobody knows when. Clarence is not satisfied with the message; he wants more precision, and as he presses the old woman with questions, she falls to the ground in an erotic frenzy with her snakes. Prisoner of the big snake, the protagonist is obliged to stay and watch. To set his eyes on something other than the disgusting spectacle of Dioki's erotic trance, he looks up to the sky and has a clear vision of the coming of the King; in fact it is a reenactment of the esplanade scene, but the King is leaving the palace instead of disappearing into it. The vision is so vivid, and the King seems so close, that Clarence tries to catch his eye, hoping to make contact, to exist for the King even for a fleeting moment, but the monarch's blank and indifferent expression chills him to the bone. A great cry is heard and the vision disappears. Dioki gets up and the snakes leave her gently. She then tells Clarence, "Now you know . . . go then, leave me." But as he is about to leave, she says, laughing ironically, "Know that no woman is ever so old that she cannot be ill-treated."⁵⁸

The divination scene with Dioki takes the narrative into the final, spiritual phase. It does so by announcing the imminent arrival of the King, and by dehumanizing the sexual act, therefore shifting its importance from the expression of human desire and self-indulgence to that of a cosmic force. Laye reintroduces the allegorical image of the snake, but here again enlarges the symbolism. As in its previous manifestations in *L'Enfant noir* and *Dramouss,* the snake is once more the messenger of the supernatural world. It is an intermediary, bridging the gap between two realities; through the voice of the soothsayer, it dispenses knowledge otherwise out of human reach. It also represents a threat, a danger that Clarence willingly faces for a chance to hear about the King, thus proving his good-will and his strong desire for new life. Finally, it is the African phallic and erotic symbol of fecundity rites. And it is the union of the snake and the old woman that brings on the lifelike vision of the coming of the King.

The entire scene is heavy with ambiguous sexual overtones. Before meeting the old woman, Clarence was told that "she pickled her nose" ("elle se pique le nez") although not with wine, but with her snakes. Knowing this, the protagonist's speech is spiced with double entendres, perfectly well understood by Dioki, when, for example, she tells him that he must not ill-treat her in any way. The expression in itself does not usually have any sexual connotations, but it does in this context, as proven by Clarence's sarcastic reply and Dioki's ironic statement that a woman is never too old to be mistreated. Although the protagonist has witnessed the coupling of Dioki and her snakes, a possibility arises in his mind that perhaps he himself took the place of the snakes and made love to the old hag; this distressing intuition is reinforced by the two boys, who say they saw Dioki embracing him. The situation is never clarified, and purposely so; to keep up the dreamlike and sensual atmosphere that permeates the book, and further to underline the ritualistic intent of the scene. The fish-women represented desire and sensuality, but Dioki is the antithesis of sexual appeal. Clarence finds her ugly and makes a clear distinction between her and the women of the village:

He could never manage to see a woman's face, except through the narrow frame of a window, but as for Dioki, he could see her perfectly well. As for the others, when he met them, he only saw their breasts or their buttocks; he could not unglue his eyes from their breasts or their rump; but in Dioki's case, he was aware of the entire body. Her breasts were so withered that one could not bring oneself to look at them; as for her buttocks, they had disappeared; one could have sworn she had no bottom left at all.[59]

Dioki is no longer a woman for Clarence, and the sexual act that took place, whether with the snakes or with his own participation, must be seen as a religious ritual like the elemental union that activates the forge. Hierogamy is always ritualistic in Africa, and the sexual trance that takes place at the bottom of the pit releases energies favorable to the foretelling of the future and ensuring its realization. The vision of the King coming to Aziana is projected onto a ceiling high above the pit where Dioki is mating with the snakes, and may thus represent the polarization of human nature: the beast and the angel. Laye reinforces the antithesis through the use of colors: the pit is dark and dusty, and the ceiling red and full of sunlight. Clarence is once more confronted with the two sides of his nature, and, through self-disgust, takes one step closer to the realization of his quest.

Laye insists in this scene on the visual element and uses the eyes as a metaphor for knowledge. Clarence goes into the soothsayer's pit to see the future, and as the boy had told him, he will not see anything if he does not take the trouble to look. Conversely to the long dream near the river, Clarence is not dreaming now, and is not drugged by the odor of the South. He is held under the cold gaze of the snake and watches everything intensely, unable to move for fear of being bitten, alive only through his eyes. He sees Dioki as he has never seen a woman before, he sees her monstrous embrace, he sees the King and most of all he sees the expression in the King's eyes. This emphasis on seeing sets the mood for the final episode when Clarence hopes that the King will look upon him. The whole metaphor is most likely Sufi in origin, and Laye's meaning is well expressed by Plotinus, whose teaching influenced Sufism: "the eye would not be able to see the sun if, in a manner, it were not itself a sun. Given that the sun is the source of light, and that light is symbolic of the intelligence and of the spirit, then the process of seeing represents a spiritual act and symbolizes understanding."[60] This insistence on the visual reappears in Laye's short story Les Yeux de la statue, although in this case the metaphor remains obscure and sheds no light on the meaning of the story.

Le Regard du Roi. After leaving Dioki's pit, Clarence is told that the King will arrive the next day, around noon. As the hero comes closer to his goal, Laye concentrates the themes and images of the novel around the central figure of the King, harmoniously blending together the form and the content of the book, and thus making the novel into a metaphor for the Islamic dogma of Unity. "Islamic art seeks always to relate the multiplicity of forms, shapes and colors to the One, to the Center and Origin, thereby reflecting tawhîd (unity) in its own way in the world of forms with which it is concerned."[61]

In the last hours that separate him from the fulfillment of his dream, Clarence is assaulted by self-doubt and the tormenting feeling of his moral inadequacy. He reflects upon his life in Aziana and the role he has played in the village, above all his convenient blindness to what was happening and then his acceptance of it, as if it were impossible to change things, thus revealing his taste and his attraction for the "unmentionable." Although the end is near, the struggle is not over and the last obstacle comes through the Master of Ceremonies. He comes to inform Clarence that the Naba has decided that he must not leave his hut, and will have to watch the ceremonies intended for the King through his windows. Upon hearing this, everything collapses for Clarence, because it means that although he will see the King, the King will not see him. It means there is no way out of Aziana and out of the life he has been leading for so long. It means there is no more hope. Clarence protests and sends Samba Baloum to ask the Naba to reverse his order and he succeeds, but the Master of Ceremonies has succeeded also in destroying Clarence's courage and faith in the King's mercy. Unable to stop him from participating in the ceremonies, he demonstrates to the hero that he is totally unworthy of the King, and his hope of seeing him is nothing more than foolish arrogance. " 'A cock! That's all you are,' he said. 'It is as a cock the beggar sold you to the Naba, and it is as a cock you've behaved! . . . A cock is not worthy to appear before the King,' said the master of ceremonies. 'Loathsome as you are, you are good for nothing but the harem!' "[62]

As for the Master of Ceremonies, it is in his heart that he carries his foulness, for he symbolizes the self-righteous hypocrite, blind to his own weaknesses, full of his own importance, proud to serve the Naba, who represents nothing more than human justice in all its imperfection and cruelty. To comfort Clarence, Samba Baloum, who in many ways speaks for the author, tells him, ". . . Nabas are a dime a dozen. The King is here, and the Naba is nobody, the Naba is less than dog's dung."[63]

But Clarence's will is broken and his shame overwhelms him. The depth of his sorrow is such that once again the memory of the violent surf fills his mind. He no longer hears the drums announcing the King but the bellowing of the ocean. The initial threat of the great bar protecting the African coast comes back to haunt him; Laye reintroduces the image drawn from the beginning of the novel and symbolizing the quest, to close out the metaphor now as the voyage comes to its end. The plight that Clarence experienced in crossing the bar is now enlarged to represent the plight of humanity and the difficulty of life. Laye is saying that we are all in the same boat, eager to cross the bar and to come ashore, not understanding that it would have been better to be engulfed by the ocean, or never to have been born, for the moment we land on the red soil of Africa, that is, of life, the difficulty begins and the long path to salvation must now be traveled. This pessimism toward life is deep-rooted in Laye and commensurate with his faith in God.

In *L'Enfant noir,* upon learning of a friend's death, the protagonist says, "I think that Check has preceded us on God's path . . . which is certainly less frightening than the other . . . the path of life . . . which is never anything more than the temporary path of our exile."[64] The image and sound of the ocean are replaced by the bestial cries of the two youths dancing a fecundity dance, a dance they have rehearsed many times in preparation for the King's arrival. The incident brings back the theme of lust and sensuality, and

Clarence felt the blood of shame enflaming his cheeks . . . but was it up to him to blush? Had he been offended? . . . He had not always been blushing, he had himself been an actor in this dance and he was not ashamed then; . . . but why had this ritual mime been chosen to show the King? Was it not going to give offense to the King? Insult his purity? Or was it that the mere presence of the King would purify the ritual dance? . . . Could it be that the King's presence would suffice to purify everything?[65]

Clarence cannot bring himself to believe this and decides he will remain in his hut as the Naba had suggested. This decision brings on the protestation of his friends, and allows the author to plead his case for man's salvation.

The arguments presented through the different protagonists have definite Sufi overtones, and although some of the ideas put forth seem Christian in their nature, it must be pointed out that Sufism was inspired by both Neo-Platonic thought and Christianity, while remaining subordinate to an Islamic structure of ideas. Clarence feels unworthy of the King because of the sinful life he has led, and he is convinced that nothing can wash away the impurities that stain his soul. To this, the Naba's eunuch, Samba Baloum, retorts, "You are as worthy as anyone else. If all those who present themselves to the King had to be worthy of him, the King would live in a desert."[66] In his societal role, Samba Baloum is the antithesis of Clarence, but in the eyes of God they are both men of good-will and deserving of divine Mercy. Diallo, the blacksmith, is also optimistic and confident in the infinite mercy of the King. " 'It is always too late,' said Diallo. 'We are hardly born, that it is already too late. But the King knows this, and that is why it is never too late.' "[67] As for himself, his only merit is to have forged an axe, a simple axe, and this is what represents his worth, his lifetime work. In this, the blacksmith exemplifies the Sufi doctrine that "through the process of making things the artisan has been able to achieve spiritual perfection and inner integration, thanks to the bond created between the guilds and the Sufi orders. The transformation of color, shape and other accidents that materials undergo in the hand of the artisan came to possess a symbolic significance connected with the transformation of the human soul."[68]

Just as Alchemy became the link between Sufism and art, and consequently between art and the divine, Diallo in his pursuit of the perfect axe is in fact trying to reach God. But Clarence is not an artisan; he is even poorer than if he had had nothing, because he has the stench of his sins. At the end of his long journey, Clarence has lost all pride and self-esteem; he is naked spiritually and physically. The only thing he has managed to sustain and which in turn has sustained him is his undeniable desire to see the King, the blind faith that his salvation rests with him, and all his good-will has been devoted to reaching that goal. As in Sufism, Clarence's ideal is not virtue, because virtue is not an end in itself but only a means of uniting with God: to know God one must know oneself, and to know oneself is somehow to know evil, for good and evil are inevitably linked in man's nature. However, Clarence's humility stops him from understanding this and he remains unconvinced by the arguments of his well-wishers, and all seems lost.

The final scene is totally dominated by Sufi mysticism and its metaphorical language. All Sufi texts discuss the different "stations" and "states" the individual must go through to achieve his union with God. However, they exhibit vast differences in the nuances of meaning attached to the two words as well as to how many of each "phase" are necessary to unite with the divine. It is evident that Laye does not follow one specific Sufi master, but rather uses what fits his purpose while nevertheless remaining faithful to the overall doctrine. Most Sufis accept that "the term 'station' denotes the way of the seeker, and his prayers in the field of exertion, and his rank before God in proportion to his merit; the term 'state' denotes the favor and grace which God bestows upon the heart of his servant, and which are not connected with any mortification on the latter's part."[69] The last moments of Clarence's quest are examined in light of this definition.

After his friends' final admonition to seize his chances and present himself to the King, Clarence falls suddenly into semiconsciousness, in which he can hear what is going on, and even see himself participating in the conversation, but at the same time he is detached from it, removed from reality. The whole incident is like "something which resembles life . . . something which was perhaps life itself: a pure folly and a saraband of fools!"[70] How long he remains in this semiconsciousness is not specified, but when he comes to, he is totally alone and naked in his hut amidst a very deep silence. "Is this the way one dies, he asked himself in a low voice. Without a doubt it was the way . . . one entered into a diffuse light, a soft and strong light . . . but where did the light come from . . . then he saw the King."[71] This deathlike "station" experienced by the protagonist means that he has detached himself from the world, following the advice of the Prophet, "die before you die," and turned away from the flesh in order to enter the spiritual world.

Looking up at the radiance of the King from the narrow window, Clarence is once again anguished by his foulness and, feeling he has lost everything, wishes he could live his life over. His distress is somewhat eased by the thought that he may have lacked virtue but never good-will. He never liked his sinful ways, and always wished to be good. He was always ashamed of the beast in him, and his hope was always turned toward the King. This is how he has sought God; these are his meager deeds and his only merit. Painfully aware of the paucity of his accomplishments, "tears sprang from his eyes": at that very moment the King's eyes fall upon him and seem to call him. Clarence's regret and tears of repentance can be seen as the last station before entering the state of grace that the King has bestowed upon him. Hypnotized and transfixed by the King's gaze, he moves toward him, naked as he is, miraculously going through the walls of the hut, drawn as by an irresistible force and pierced by the King's gaze as by a fiery blade:

When he stood before the King, when he stood in the great radiance of the King, still overwhelmed by the blade of fire, but living and living only thanks to that fire, Clarence fell upon his knees, for it finally came to him that he was at the end of his quest, and at the end of all quests.

But surely he had still not come quite close enough; he was perhaps still too timid, for the King opened his arms to him. And as he opened his arms, his cloak opened slightly and revealed his slender adolescent torso. On this torso, in the midnight of this slender torso there appeared—at the center— but not quite at the center . . . a little to the right—a faint pulsating under the skin. It was this beating, this faint pulsation which was calling! It was this fire which was burning, and this light which was radiating upon him. It was this love which was all-consuming—

"Didn't you know I was waiting for you?" asked the King.

And Clarence gently placed his lips upon the faint and yet immense beating of that heart. Then the King slowly closed his arms and his vast mantle, enveloping Clarence for ever.[72]

This final ecstatic scene brings to mind a text from the twelfth-century thinker Ahmad Ghazali, whose book on Pure Love, that is, divine love, is a classic of Sufi mysticism:

When love truly exists, the lover becomes the nourishment of the Beloved; it is not the Beloved who is the nourishment of the lover, because the Beloved cannot be contained into the lover . . . The butterfly which has become the lover of the flame, has for sole nourishment, as long as it is still a distance away, the light of the dawn. It is the foretelling sign of the morning illumination which calls him and welcomes him. But he must continue to fly until he has joined it. When he has arrived, it is no longer up to him to progress toward the flame, it is the flame that progresses in him. It is not the flame that is his nourishment, but he himself that is the nourishment of the flame. For a fugitive moment he himself becomes the Beloved (since he is the flame) and this is the perfection of love.[73]

The similarity of the two texts is interesting, although it is not to be inferred that Laye was inspired directly by this particular text; indeed he may not even have been aware of it. He was, however, certainly cognizant of the Sufi mystical conception of divine love and of the metaphorical language used to express it. Among the great variety of images that can be found in Sufi mystical poetry and essays, the images of fire and light are a constant.

The closing scene of the novel has raised speculation on the part of the critics, particularly as to the exact meaning of the King's embrace. Does it symbolize the spiritual ascension of the hero, or his death, as in Ch. H. Kane's novel *L'Aventure ambiguë?* This latter interpretation strikes us as unsatisfactory, for we view Laye's novel as a deeply optimistic book. Unlike Kane's hero, Clarence has no cultural contradictions. In fact, at the end of the story, he has become more African than the natives. Moreover, there is no indication, anywhere in the text, that he misses his native culture or is in any way torn between his past and his present situations. Furthermore, the epigraph of the book, taken from Kafka's *Aphorism 13*, ". . . The

Lord will pass through the corridor and looking at the prisoner will say: 'This one must not be locked up anymore: he is coming to me,' " announces the salvation of the hero and thus clearly accentuates the positive spirit which animates the novel. In fact, as Ben Obumselu points out, Laye refutes Kafka's pessimistic view of our human destiny by quoting only part of the text, thus reversing its original negative meaning and affirming his own optimism. Laye's purposes are religious and universal, the eternal odyssey of man's search for God and salvation, and the reassuring thought that in the presence of God's infinite mercy and all-encompassing love, all men are equal and all may be saved.

Another speculation, this one not so easily answered, concerns the image of God as a fragile adolescent African king. It certainly does not mesh with Islamic orthodoxy, and seems to be the antithesis of the Christian God. J. J. Achiriga speculates that it may be an effort on Laye's part to rehabilitate African values and to insist on the fact that many African religions recognize the existence of a supreme God, therefore refuting the argument that Africans are primitive because they are not monotheist. It could also be argued that, once more, it is the Sufis who provide a possible interpretation of Laye's image, and in particular those who professed the esoteric doctrine of divine love. In this particular school of thought, one controversial tendency concerns the anthropomorphism of the Beloved. However, this possibility must not be allowed to overshadow the author's private mythology. He does insist on the color of the skin, and the blank expression of the King's face, reminiscent of Benin and Ifé statuary, thus giving a definite African-ness to the divine. It may be that for Laye, God was African, or as Adèle King so aptly points out, Laye felt that "in God's sight we are all Africans."[74]

To conclude this analysis of Laye's important novel, let us emphasize once more the originality of the metaphorical language. It is a genuine tour de force of cultural integration in the highest and most positive sense of the word. The imaginary universe created by the author has the fascination of mythology and the universal appeal of human wisdom.

Chapter Five
Le Maître de la parole

Introduction

Camara Laye's last work, *Le Maître de la parole (The Guardian of the Word)*, was published in 1978 and the following year received Le Prix de l'Académie Française. The book completes and reinforces the positive image of Africa that *L'Enfant noir* had presented to the world twenty-five years earlier. In an interview, the author underlined the spiritual connection between the two works and stated that his intent was to "restore Africa in all its beauty and all its truth, and not in the debasement she may have known."[1]

It is interesting to note that *L'Enfant noir* begins with a dedicatory poem to the African mother and *Le Maître de la parole* with a poem singing the black soul, the African soul that is the spirit of a race and of a continent. Laye's works form a harmonious unity in which the private memories of an individual lead and finally blend into the memories of his people.

The book was very well received by the press and the reviews were unanimously positive, but it does not yet appear to have been the subject of serious critical analysis; Adèle King's book on Laye's writings, in which she devotes a small chapter to *Le Maître de la parole*, remains to this day the most extensive critical treatment of the work.

Le Maître de la parole is not an original work, in that Laye did not invent the story or the language but transcribed and translated a version of a Mali epic, the *Soundiata*, as it was told to him by the famous griot Babou Condé. However, it is more than a transcription and Laye's rendition of the poem reflects quite overtly the style and vision of the "scribe." It is the work of a poet, not of a historian, and as such stands as a statement on contemporary Africa and a poetic vision of the mother land, much as *The Song of Roland* can be seen as poetic testimony on twelfth-century French feudal society. Like the *Roland* it represents an ideal. For the French epic, the Christian ideal embodied by Charlemagne was particularly fitting in the twelfth cen-

tury, the time of the first crusades, and the society depicted reflects
the age of the poet, not of its heroes. Moreover, the lesson to be
drawn from Roland's hubris is intended for the appreciation and
judgment of the poet's contemporaries. Laye's *Soundiata* is also intended for his contemporaries and the Malinké ideal (contrary to that
of the *Roland*) is still valid. Furthermore, it is sung still in time of
trouble for Africa, in order to do what the epic has always done: give
courage and faith to those who hear it, as well as to entertain and to
teach them.

Laye's transcription of the *Soundiata* was not the first to appear in
French. In 1960, the Guinean historian Djibril Niane published
Soundjata ou l'épopée mandingue,[2] and his version was inspired primarily
by the griot Mamadou Kouyaté as well as other versions he had heard
in Malinké country. In 1970, Massa Makan Diabaté published (in
French) *Kala Jata*,[3] a version of *Soundiata* told by the griot Kele Mou-
son, and, in 1975, *L'aigle et l'épervier ou la geste de Sunjata, poème populaire*.[4] Three other versions of *Soundiata* exist in English, gathered
by Gordon Innes[5] and published in 1974; they originate from three
different Gambian griots and, like all the other versions mentioned,
reveal no major differences as to the fundamental facts of the story.
Innes believes that "the differences between versions occur at the level
of the individual griot, not of region."[6] To this Niane would add that
the different griots also belong to different schools which emphasize
and underline different details of the story, doing so for reasons
known only to themselves. However, the griot is no longer the only
one to orient the story in a certain direction, for it is important to
understand that the transcriber does, too, consciously or not.

The poem was not meant to be written, and in doing so the writer
takes on some of the art of the griot, as surely as the medieval European cleric must have done. The histrionics that accompany the re-
citation of the epic are lost in the written form; like reading a play
instead of seeing it performed, much of the magic disappears. The
writer, even if he is faithful to the bard is nevertheless transposing
intonation and expression into fixed words. He also chooses the griot
and the version that appeal to him the most, and this is done for
strictly personal reasons, since all versions are fundamentally the same
in regard to the facts; it can therefore be assumed that it is the details, the region, or the personality of the griot that influence the
writer's choice. This problem is not unique to African epics but in-
herent to the genre; it is however more evident in Africa because the

old bards are still performing, whereas in the case of the European epic, for example, we often have no idea of how it was recited, to what music, and how many versions existed before the one which came down to us.

The fact that we have access to different versions of the *Soundiata* is a great advantage in that we can obtain a fairly accurate understanding of the writer's specific contribution. In analyzing Laye's version, Niane's will be the main point of reference, as it would be superfluous in the context of this essay to compare Laye's to all the other written accounts of the legend. Laye and Niane's versions are particularly well suited to comparison, since they represent the main French transcriptions of the *Soundiata* by two Guinean intellectuals of the same generation, who consulted the same sources, encountered the same difficulties, and yet made different choices as to the version they prefer. Niane is a historian and his intentions are different from Laye's; he is mostly interested in the historical evidence of the epic and has chosen the version of a specific region because that is where the ancient city of Niani was located and where he had himself participated in an archaeological expedition on site. Laye is a poet, mostly concerned with the image of Africa which appears in filigree behind the life and deeds of the hero; he also had a personal interest in the epic, since he claims that one of his ancestors, Fran Camara, helped Soundiata in the conquest of Mali.

The Empire of Mali

It is the Arabs who have for the most part written the history of Medieval Africa, and up to the fifteenth century there was a great deal of communication between the north and the south of the Sahara. The great empires of the Western Sudan rose and fell between the fourth and the fifteenth centuries, and Mali or Manden was one of them. Sudanese civilization started to decline around the fifteenth century with the Portuguese explorations, under the blows of the slave trade and the use of firearms. The empire of Mali came into being at the fall of the empire of Ghana in the eleventh century. The historian Ibrahima Baba Kake distinguishes four great periods in the history of Mali: "1) From its origins to the 13th century. 2) The Empire of Soundiata and its successors. 3) The golden age of the Empire, the 15th century. 4) The beginning of the decline, 15th–16th century."[7]

Soundiata was the founder of the Empire of Mali, uniting the different kingdoms of the Manden under his rule. At the beginning of the thirteenth century, Mali was only a small kingdom, a vassal-state of the Sosso kingdom, whose king was Suomaoro. The legend of Soundiata as we know it today originated in the seventeenth century, when the empire was well into its decline. Niane feels that the creation of a Soundiata cycle "was the first effort to provide the Malinké aristocracy with a reassuring image of itself and the world. It is an effort on their part to negate time, and the establishment of a decadent classicism: the contemplation of an ideal and idealized past."[8] Nothing is known of the Soundiata legend before the seventeenth century. Before Soundiata, the kings of the Manden were Moslem and two of them had been to Mecca; but it was under Soundiata that the Empire of Mali put itself resolutely under the banner of Islam. However, *Soundiata* is wholly animist in spirit and, surprisingly, Islam plays a very limited role in the epic. Niane and Laye mention that Soundiata is dressed like a Moslem king, and the presence of the marabouts is indicated several times, but in Niane this is the extent of the hero's "islamization." Laye, for reasons to be discussed below, insists more on the Islamic content. Ibrahima Kake is of the opinion that Soundiata captured popular imagination because he remained faithful to the animist beliefs of his ancestors; this would also explain why the tradition ignores the majority of Soundiata's immediate successors. The legend of Soundiata is part of a greater cycle which constitutes the common tradition of all the Malinké. According to Niane, the cycle or corpus of Soundiata is composed as follows:

(1) The genesis of the Manden from its beginning to Soundiata, the Keita (the royal family) are supposed to descend from Bilal, the first black muezzin of Islam. (It is also said that he served the Prophet personally.)

(2) The genealogy of all the companions of Soundiata, artificially linked to biblical characters or Islamic saints.

(3) The story of Soundiata or "Soundjata Fassa" which gives its name to the cycle. It deals with the military deeds of Soundiata and his principal generals.

(4) Several epic songs which constitute the great Malinké music.

(5) The political and social constitution of the Empire.

(6) The list of the sixteen Malinké clans and of the five Marabou clans of the Mali.

(7) The mores and customs of the time of Soundiata.[9]

The epic of Soundiata is told everywhere in Malinké country, but, according to the region, the griots emphasize different parts of the cycle or different characters.

The Griot

The griots as genealogists, storytellers, musicians, and traditionalists, as they are called today, are found all over West Africa. The origin of the word *griot* is unknown and could be European or African. The word first appears in France in seventeenth-century travel accounts, and is often spelled "guiriot," but it is mentioned by Arab travelers as early as the fifteenth century. In Malinké, the word "griot" is translated by two words: *jeli,* which means "blood," in reference to the legendary origin of the griots, and *jali,* which could be a simple difference of pronunciation. According to Hugo Zemp, Jeli is the older form, but the argument is still open to conjecture. There is also another category of griots, called *Fina,* and they differ from the others in that they do not play any musical instrument. In traditional Malinké society, which is clanic, organized into castes, and respectful of a rigid hierarchy, the griot belongs to a special caste, that of the *nyamakala,* which is considered an inferior caste. The two other castes are the *horo* or "noble," and the *jon* or "prisoners" and "slaves." Among the *nyamakala* the griots are the only ones who do not have a trade. They enjoy many immunities in traditional society; in time of war, for example, they cannot be captured or enslaved. In daily social interaction, they cannot be insulted or threatened and are never subject to the death penalty. They can visit anyone they please, and always receive something for their performance however unwanted it may have been. The griots are the only ones in society to receive without ever having to give. There are many legends about the origin of the griots, and some of them explain the ambiguous position they occupy in society, although no one specific reason has yet been totally accepted by scholars. Their ambiguous societal situation is not without parallel to that of women.[10] The griots practice the art of speaking, and as Laye points out, "The word was a feminine art solely reserved to griots and women."[11] In fact, the woman and the griot are two fundamental sources of Malinké oral literature. However, female griots, or griottes, are not allowed to sing the genealogies or transmit the public speeches of the notable men in society.

According to Niane, and in this Laye concurs, the oral tradition of

the Manden is kept up by different teaching centers sometimes referred to as griots' school. Although the different centers have their
own peculiarities, they all gravitate around the Soundiata cycle. Camara Laye chose the version of the school of Fadama, a small village
of the Upper Niger, about five kilometers from Kouroussa. Tradition
is upheld by the Condé, a griot clan formed in the fifteenth century
"who retain the monopoly of the teaching of the tradition for the
Southern Savannah."[12] Laye consulted the griot Babou Condé from 16
March to 16 April 1963, during which time the griot explained that
the tradition of Fadama has four categories of the Word, of which the
first is "Kouma Lafolo Kouma," the story of Soundiata. Babou
Condé, who died in 1964, was a very famous griot and a fine Arabic
scholar. He was a *Bélën-Tigui* or "Master of the Word." "He held the
chair of history for all the regions around Kouroussa, and these regions count around one hundred thousand souls."[13] Here is his version of *Soundiata*.

The epic begins, "There were two hunters" . . . two brothers, the
elder, Moké Moussa, and the younger, Moké Dantouman. They were
great hunters and also had great magical powers. They heard that the
kingdom of Dô was devastated and terrorized by a buffalo. Of course,
they did not know that the buffalo was the ancestral totem of the
king of Dô's sister, Dô-Kamissa. At the death of their father, Dô-
Kamissa's brother became king and cheated his sister of her inheritance. Offended and bitter, Dô-Kamissa left the capital and founded
her own village a few miles away. She decided to avenge herself by
taking the form of her totem and destroying and trampling the fields
and rice-paddies of the kingdom, killing all the hunters who tried to
approach her. Attempting to end this calamity, the king promised
the most beautiful girl in his kingdom to the one who would kill the
buffalo.

Before leaving to hunt the buffalo, the two young hunters, being
Malinké, consulted a soothsayer. He told them they would be victorious if they followed his advice: first, not to answer anyone's call
while on their way, second, to befriend a little old woman they
would find near the river, for she was the answer to their problem,
and finally, after killing the buffalo, to choose for a wife the ugliest
girl in all the kingdom of Dô. They observed the first condition without any difficulty and found the old lady as foretold. The older
brother, Moké Moussa, went ahead to announce their arrival to the
king, and the younger, Moké Dantouman, stayed and befriended the

old woman. She told him who she was, and gave him three magic objects: a distaff, a flat stone, and an egg, with which he would succeed in killing the beast, if he followed her instructions. Moké Dantouman went to where the buffalo was and, upon seeing it, aimed three times at it before using his bow. The beast started chasing him, and when it got too close the hunter threw the distaff behind him and a forest of bamboo sprang out of the earth. The buffalo had to cross it slowly, but soon regained its speed; as it drew closer, the hunter threw the flat stone and it became a huge maze, which again slowed the animal. Finally, as it was again nearly upon the young man, he threw the egg, which turned into a large muddy pond in which the buffalo got stuck, whereupon the hunter killed it. The older brother, who, in cowardly fashion, had observed everything from a tall tree, came down and sang his brother's deeds, and then they went to see the king.

The old woman had warned the victor that the ugly girl he was to pick would be seated on top of a mirador, and if he could make her his wife she would bear him a very famous son. Disdaining all the pretty girls waiting to be chosen, he went to the one seated on the mirador, whose name was Sogolon Condé. She was a hunchback with large bulging eyes, and when he chose her, the crowd ridiculed him and thought him mad. Humiliated by the experience, the two hunters and the girl left the kingdom of Dô for their native Manden. It was a long journey, and the first night they stopped in a village, where they found food and shelter. The winner told his older brother that, following custom, he was to marry first, and therefore must go into Sogolon's hut. The young woman was already asleep, but when he lay beside her, she instinctively called upon her double, a porcupine, and all the hair on her body turned into quills, and it was impossible to touch her. Disappointed and somewhat vexed, the young man informed his brother of his failure and encouraged him to try his luck in turn. The next night, the younger brother, upon entering Sogolon's hut, fell into a heavy sleep until the next morning. The brothers understood that Sogolon was not for them and they took her to Niani, the capital of the kingdom, to see the king.

Farakô Maghan, the beautiful, was king of the Manden. He belonged to a powerful dynasty, for his ancestor Bilali Ibn Ka Mâma had served the Prophet. One afternoon, when he was seated as usual under a great Bombax tree, a hunter from the country of Dô came to town. The hunters from Dô are known for their powers of divination, and the king's griot asked him to tell the future. The hunter threw some cowries on the sand and told the king, "By Allah, the girl who will come, flanked by two young men; you must marry her! She will give birth to a son who will impose his will on all the countries of the Savannah . . . He shall render the name of the Manden immortal."[14] Many moons went by after the hunter's prediction, but one afternoon, as the king was sitting as usual under the great tree, in the presence of his beautiful wife, Fatoumata Bérété, the awaited trio arrived. The young men told the story of the buffalo and all they knew about Sogolon Condé. The king decided to marry her and ordered a great feast. Fatoumata Bérété had great difficulty in accepting her husband's marriage, and despite the king's reiterations of love, jealousy festered in her heart. On the wedding night, Sogolon showed the same resistance that she had previously demonstrated. The king, upset and humiliated, consulted the future by throwing river stones on the ground, which is the way of the Malinké hunters. He read that Sogolon had to be subdued by terror, so he pretended that he wanted to kill her: terrorized, the young woman consented to the consummation of the marriage, and Soundiata was conceived that very night.

All went well between the king and Sogolon, but Fatoumata's jealousy increased daily. She had given two children to the king, a boy and a girl, and she feared for her son's right to the throne. She tried all kinds of magic, and consulted many witches to harm Sogolon, but to no avail. One Monday in January 1202, after a terrible tornado, Sogolon gave birth to a boy. He was named Mari (emir) Diata (lion), Naré Maghan Diata (name of his father), Sogolon Diata (name of his mother). He inherited the totems of his parents, the lion from his father and the buffalo and the panther from his mother. His father gave him a griot who was none other than the son of the king's own griot, Balla Fassali Kouyaté. The child was called by everyone Sogolon-Diata, which quickly became Soundiata.

After the promises of glory which preceded his birth, the boy was a terrible disappointment to his parents and a sheer triumph to Fatoumata. He was crippled and could not use his legs; Sogolon bore two other children to the king, a boy and a girl. The king took a third wife, a Camara with whom he had a son, Nan Boukari, who later became Soundiata's right arm. The king died and Fatoumata's son, Dankaran Touman, succeeded him. Time passed and Soundiata, although five years old (the exact age varies with the versions), still could not use his legs. Each day, his mother had to face the sarcasm and cruel remarks of Fatoumata, now all powerful. One day, Sogolon, in need of baobab leaves to spice her meal, went to Fatoumata to ask her for some. The latter remarked that Sogolon's son should be able to fetch some for her. Humiliated, Sogolon went home and cried in despair of ever seeing her son fulfill the promises of his birth.

Soundiata, touched by his mother's sorrow and perhaps because his time had come, asked his brother to go to the blacksmith and fetch the biggest iron bar the smith could give him. The bar was so heavy that it had to be carried by several men and attracted a lot of attention. Planting the bar in the ground and using it as a cane, Soundiata raised himself to his feet, to the stupefaction of the people of Niani and the joy of his mother and friends. Then he went toward a baobab, uprooted it, and took it whole to his mother saying, "Mother . . . from now on, it is from you that the women of Niani, Fatoumata included, will get their baobab leaves."[15] From that moment on, Soundiata grew up like a normal child.

After his circumcision, he learned to hunt and spent much time in the bush. It was while he was away on a hunting expedition that his brother, Dankaran Touman, the king, sent Soundiata's griot Balla Fassali as ambassador to Sosso, kingdom of the terrible king Soumaoro. When he heard of the deed, Soundiata became furious and had a violent fight with his brother, after which he decided to leave the Manden and go into exile, but swearing to return one day. Soundiata was then about twelve. The exile took him and his family far away from the motherland, and they had four hosts before settling in Mema, near Timbuktu, where the king Moussa Tounkara treated Soundiata like his son and the heir to his throne.

Soundiata had been in exile for six years and was now a young man of eighteen, when Soumaoro invaded the Manden and destroyed the city of Niani. Fatoumata's son fled instead of fighting, and "the Manden was left without a master." Soumaoro was a very powerful king and his kingdom had come into existence three hundred years after the death of the Prophet. The founder of the kingdom was a blacksmith. Soumaoro was the son of Diarra Diarrasso and his three wives, for each one of them had carried him in her womb, and when he was born all of them had felt the birth pangs. He was a great sorcerer and had sixty-three totems, which rendered him almost invulnerable. His cruelty was legendary, and his political power was based on terror. Soundiata's brother, afraid of Soumaoro, had given him his sister,

Nâna Triban, in marriage. She seduced the old king by her beauty
and sensuality and became his favorite. She discovered his taboo: he
could be killed only by the spur of a white cock. Knowing his secret,
Nâna Triban waited for an opportunity to escape from the kingdom
of Sosso. Soundiata's griot was still at the court of Soumaoro and had
conquered the king by his ability to play the royal xylophone and
singing the king's praises on it. Soumaoro decided to keep the griot
as his own, thus increasing Soundiata's anger.

Under the evil rule of Soumaoro, the people of Manden remembered the prophecy, that a prince with three totems would make the
Manden glorious, and they remembered Soundiata. A search party
was sent to all the royal cities of the Savannah to find him. When
they found him in the city of Mema, he was anxious and eager to go
to fight Soumaoro. Sogolon, who had been ailing for some time,
died, having accomplished her destiny. The time had come for Soundiata to fulfill his. With no difficulty, he raised an enormous army,
as many kingdoms wanted the end of Soumaoro's rule. Among the
allies was Fran Camara (an ancestor of Camara Laye) and Fakoli Ko-
roma, Soumaoro's own nephew, who turned against his uncle because
the latter had stolen his wife, thereby committing incest.

The first battle was something of a defeat because, although the
army of Soumaoro had been beaten, the king was invulnerable and
appeared and disappeared on the battlefield at will. Soundiata was
discouraged by the magnitude of Soumaoro's powers, but shortly after
the battle, the hero's griot Fassali Kouyaté and Nâna Triban, his half-
sister and wife of the evil king, arrived at the camp, having escaped
from the enemy kingdom. Thus, Soundiata learned of Soumaoro's taboo. The decisive battle took place at Kirina, where the eighteen-
year-old Soundiata, twelfth king of the Manden, defeated the old and
powerful king Soumaoro, whose sixty-three totems abandoned him
when Soundiata grazed him with a wooden arrow headed with the
spur of a white cock. Feeling his strength and power leaving him,
Soumaoro fled the field and took refuge in the cave of Koulikoro,
from which he never again came out.

Soumaoro's defeat gave rise to great festivities, and Soundiata was
proclaimed emperor of the Manden and took the title of Mansa. He
organized it as a federation of kingdoms united under his rule, and
called it Mali, the hippopotamus, an animal as powerful on land as
in the water. Thus was born the empire of Mali. Soundiata rebuilt
the city of Niani and gave political and social structure to the empire.

He went to war again and won, and in Laye's version it is said that he died voluntarily, in the waters of the river Gambia. Niane claims that many versions say that the Mansa drowned in the river Sankarani, but the circumstances are not known. He further reports one of Delafosse's versions in which Soundiata was killed by an arrow in a public manifestation in Niani. But to this day, nobody really knows how Soundiata died, and the griots, if they know, are silent.[16]

The African Epic

Although the very existence of the African epic as a literary genre has been contested by scholars such as Sir Maurice Bowra[17] and Ruth Finnegan,[18] the weight of evidence suggests the contrary. Prominent critics such as Lilyan Kesteloot, Robert Pageard, and Isidore Ikpewho[19] acknowledge the existence of the African epic and give it its rightful place in world literature:

> The African epic possesses, in fact, all the characteristics of the traditional epic genre: not only the indispensable historical foundation, with its deviations due to the embellishment of the facts, the desire to please the prince, the popular imagination and the distance of time, but again the intervention of the fantastic, from the blowing up of the exploits and the hero's strength to the personal cooperation of the gods. Here, the sorcerers and the animal-totems replace the saints and the angels.[20]

Kesteloot goes on to say that the structure of the African epic conforms fully to that of the traditional genre in that it is a long poem lasting several hours, sung or declaimed and sustained by musical accompaniment. This is perhaps not entirely the case, however, for the African epic is rarely in verse (Finnegan's main argument). It is generally agreed that the language of the African epic, and Malinké is a prime example, is not a specifically literary language, and, as Okpewho remarks, "the prosodic structure of the song (especially in a public performance) is treated as loosely as possible, so as to give the performing bard sufficient freedom to attend to music, dance, drama, and so on, and even allow impromptu repartee and other participation from the audience."[21]

Once the epic is written down, it is usually written in prose and it is the language of the writer that must be examined, just as one might discuss the literary merit of a translation rather than its accuracy; there is ultimately no way of knowing how closely the transcriber follows the griot's text. Laye, in fact, considered *Le Maître de la parole* as an "exercise de style," an attempt to make an ancient legend seem real to the reader, and comprehensible even to children. It is thus evident, as Adèle King points out, that in this work Laye "attempts to fulfill the role of the griot in a modern context and for a modern audience."[22] He wants to entertain and to teach, and although the images are drawn from an ancient world, the lesson is meant to apply to contemporary society. Okpewho feels that "of all the devices that the bard employs to make his tale as intimate and as down-to-earth as possible, perhaps the most esthetically effective is the tendency to weave his personality into that of his characters: to give us the benefit of his judgement, or to so mesh his voice with his material that it is difficult to tell where dialogue ends and narration resumes."[23] This is certainly true of Laye, and he uses the old epic to his own ends, to present his own vision of the world. It also must be noted that, unlike Niane and even the other versions of the *Soundiata*, Laye's title does not reflect the hero of the poem but rather the storyteller, the guardian of the Word, teacher, messenger, and artist. Consequently, rather than analyze *Le Maître* as an African expression of the traditional epic genre, it is more useful to focus on Laye's personal treatment of the structure and the themes of the work: Laye's work is always a variation on the theme and image of Africa.

Structure

Le Maître de la parole is constructed around four sequences of events which follow each other in a somewhat linear fashion. The first is woven around the origin and childhood of the hero, the second his exile, the third, the history and rise of Soumaoro, and the fourth describes the hero's victorious homecoming. Niane's *Soundjata* presents the same composition but the four parts of the poem are roughly equal in length, except for the one dealing with Suomaoro, which is quite short. Laye's version is overwhelmingly unbalanced by the greater emphasis put on the first part of the narrative, which occupies half the poem. Moreover, unlike Niane, whose version begins with the kings of the Manden and Soundiata's father, Laye begins with the legend of the hero's mother. It would be interesting to know if Laye followed Babou Condé to the letter in this, or chose to begin as he does for some other reason. The same applies to the length and importance given to the description of the hero's childhood. Whatever the reasons, Laye's version is in perfect keeping with his thematic preoccupation with childhood and his vision of the mother as a symbol of the African continent and the homeland.

The style of *Le Maître* is in harmony with the spirit and mood of the epic. Laye begins: "Ils étaient deux chasseurs. . . ." The use of the imperfect tense puts the narrative into a distant and nondetermined past, befitting the ancient story without using the traditional European "Once upon a time" or its African equivalent. The language has the repetitive rhythm of poetic prose and many of the metaphors are manifestly Laye's creation and reminiscent of *Le Regard du roi*. For example, crowd descriptions in *Le Maître* are expressed by water imagery: "Soon, it was a river of raised hands . . . the children . . . mingled with the swell of the procession. . . ."[24] The story is often interrupted by songs, in the manner of the griot, and also by the interventions of the narrator, who digresses from the narrative to give an opinion or ask a question directed to the reader. It must be noted, however, that these digressions, perfectly acceptable in oral literature, are detrimental to the aesthetics of Laye's written text. They often burden the narrative with moralistic comments not easily acceptable to a modern reader. In that respect the author does not succeed in transferring smoothly the oral literary convention to the written one.

Laye often meshes his own opinions and values with those of the main characters of the story and the result is not always successful or credible as it is often anachronistic. For example, Bilali, the ancestor of the Keïta, the Malinké royal family, who for a while lived in Mecca is at one point reflecting on his situation, meaning that of a black man in the Arab world: "He realized that his deeper self was the sum of two innermost selves. The first, fashioned by his existence as a slave, was in harmony with his way of life (needing desperately to lean on his faith in the Supreme Being to subsist), was fighting the other self full of complexes and vaguely racist, hoping to be considered an equal by the Arabs if he smeared his body with ashes in order to whiten his skin."[25] This inner conflict is surely better related to the Négritude generation than to that of the ancient Malinké, for whom slavery was common practice and race inferiority complexes hardly a major issue.

All through the story, Laye brings forth messages which he considers important and crucial to his time and his contemporaries. In doing so, it is true that he fulfills the role of the griot, but good literature has its rights, and the difficulties arise when the values as well as the language of the messages are anachronistic to the mood, the style, and the characters of the legend. At times, Laye seems carried away by his message and appears deliberately to have chosen to subordinate art to the teaching of moral values. This may be explained by the fact that the author wanted to be read primarily by the general public, including children, and not necessarily by the African and European elite, and his main purpose was to teach and entertain. Also in keeping with the epic spirit are the numerous exaggerations, the accumulation of detail, and the omnipresence of the supernatural.

However, Laye departs considerably from the African traditional style of the genre in his use of psychology, in the interpretation and explanation of the characters' motives and behavior. He often treats human relationships as a modern novelist would, giving them an importance they do not usually have in the traditional text. An example is the seduction scene between Soumaoro and Nâna Triban, which is described in great detail; Laye intersperses the erotic pleasure of the couple and the expert caresses of the young woman with the explanation of her motives in a sort of stream of consciousness, through which she expresses her love of the Manden and of her people. The treatment of the scene is modern in its explicitness and in the psychological insights concerning Soumaoro's character. This modern approach to an old topic is surely done in order to please a contemporary audience. Many griots are known to spice their traditional tales with "modernisms," to amuse and more fully communicate with their public. This modernization is also evident in the interpretation of, and the light in which Laye presents, the main themes of the epic.

Childhood

There is a definite parallel between Soundiata's childhood and that of *L'Enfant noir*. The character of Sogolon Condé dominates the early years and the adolescence of Soundiata. The father, who dies early in the story, exercises very little influence on his son, and after his death he is hardly mentioned. Soundiata is his mother's son in keeping with Malinké wisdom: "Tout l'avenir d'un enfant lui vient de sa mère," says the proverb. Except for her ugliness, Sogolon Condé has a great deal in common with l'Enfant noir's mother. Although the prominence of maternal influence is common to all versions of the epic,

Laye draws a particularly strong portrait of Sogolon. It is for his mother that Soundiata accomplishes his first deed, and even if the time has come to manifest himself, he has only to stand up to start fulfilling his prophecy. The uprooting of the baobab is a very touching scene, a beautiful homage to the mother such as is rarely seen in epic literature, where the hero, if he usually acts for an ideal, is also very preoccupied by his own glory. It is his mother's tears and humiliation that gave Soundiata the courage and the incentive to take his place in society.

This importance of the mother is remarkable in a culture which by all accounts did not trust women and gave them very little power. In fact, here and there in the narrative, Laye intervenes to comment on the status of women past and present: "What was a woman in these long gone days but an object whose duty was to bring children into the world, to raise them, and who did not even have the same rights as the man when it came to inheritance. We cannot explain this clearly, although since that time, the Malinké of Sangaran have amended their ways and rehabilitated woman, placing her on the same level as man."[26]

Sogolon Condé, for her day, was an unusual maternal figure, just as the mother of l'Enfant noir stands out in contemporary fiction. They are not typical Malinké women but an idealized vision. Their lives are spent serving others but they are not subservient or passive, in fact they command respect, and although they both yield to their sons' wishes, it is not without reluctance. In *Le Maître de la parole,* it is Soundiata who decides to leave the country (in Niane, it is Sogolon) and he is apprehensive about telling his mother; he tries to have his brother break the news, but the latter answers, "No, we will have to tell her together. Believe me, it will take at least the two of us to tell her!"[27] In *L'Enfant noir,* the hero has decided to go to France and he must tell his mother; he would like his father to do the job, but the father gives the same answer as Soundiata's brother, in the exact same words: "nous ne serons pas trop de deux! Tu peux m'en croire."[28]

Sogolon Condé, like l'Enfant noir's mother, is a pillar of tradition and teaches her son the wisdom of Malinké culture, even when it is misogynist in nature. Before leaving in exile, she gives him four pieces of advice: "love your wife but do not trust her with State secrets, a king has no friend, someone else's son and someone else's country are not like one's own, a kingdom cannot function without

the help of the elders."[29] These recommendations, however (not mentioned by Niane), seem to be a literary device conceived by Laye to
introduce traditional Malinké wisdom as well as to foreshadow what
is to come. Later on Soundiata will experience the truth of these remarks, thus proving their wisdom and their value. Last, the two
mothers possess both supernatural powers and protective totems, and
have a great knowledge of the supernatural.

Soundiata, like l'Enfant noir, goes through the common experiences of all Malinké boys, that is, the terror of "Kondén Diara" or
ceremony of the lions, followed by circumcision, which they will also
endure collectively, for the ceremony is performed to allow an entire
age-group to enter adult life together. The two rituals are described
at length in L'Enfant noir, but in Le Maître de la parole Laye informs
the reader of their origin; according to Babou Condé, the ceremony
of "Kondén Diara" was introduced into Malinké society some 1,200
years ago by the fourth king of the Manden. Thus the narrator underlines the long tradition which sustains Malinké customs and the kin-
ship that unites all the participants, bonded by the same childhood
experiences and the same vision of life. This bond is stronger than
time and through it l'Enfant noir–Laye feels linked to the great Soundiata.

Laye sustains the parallel between himself and the Malinké hero
through the sorrow and anguish of exile. Soundiata, like Laye, exiles
himself voluntarily for what might be considered political reasons,
but with the firm intention to return one day. Laye lived many years
in exile, as a student in Paris and later in Senegal for political reasons. As he tells of Soundiata's first days in exile, Laye interrupts the
narrative to express nostalgia for the motherland: "The motherland,
in spite of the hospitality that one can find in other countries—the
host country ignores social rank—the motherland will always be more
than a simple country: she is the Earth!"[30] Here the nostalgia is not
the sweet sorrow of L'Enfant noir, but tinged with the bitterness of
experience; Laye adds that the motherland, imperfect as it may be,
embodies a cherished way of life that one carries within oneself, fear-
ing, however, to confront the memory with reality. This allusion to
the often difficult experience of homecoming does not apply to Soundiata, and the narrator is speaking more particularly for himself and
many of his contemporaries, thus reflecting on the present through
the medium of the past.

Order and Chaos

One of the main themes of the epic is the struggle between the forces of good and evil, embodied by Soundiata and Soumaoro. Pageard, reflecting on the legend, proposes an interesting but not too convincing interpretation of the struggle, to the effect that "the constant presence of the marabouts in the legend somewhat invests the struggle between Soundiata and Soumangouron with the character of the struggle between two countries in the process of Islamization (Ghana and Manding) against an essentially animist prince."[31] However, as mentioned above, the presence of Islam is very discreet, and Soundiata's faith is more in name than in deed. Scholars are somewhat unclear as to the hero's religious stance, but the main trend is to consider Soundiata as animist in belief, although historically he was a Moslem king. As for Soumaoro, he is considered essentially animist but it can be argued that his struggle with Soundiata does not symbolize the conflict between Islam and Animism, but rather the eternal battle between good and evil in human nature and its consequences for humanity.

The legend of Soumaoro is truly fascinating and his character very complex. He is undoubtedly an evil man with extraordinary powers due to his ancestry. He comes from a long line of royal smiths and his ancestor was the first to bring fire to the Manden. He is protected almost to the point of immortality by sixty-three totems, and in fact there is no actual proof of his death, for he simply disappears into the cave of Koulikoro.

The evil of the king has two outlets: cruelty and sensuality. His legendary savagery and ruthlessness help him maintain his political power over many, but it must be noted that it is his sensuality, a weakness of character, that brings him to his downfall. Laye insists at length on the sensuality of the old king and his lustful passion for his young wife, Nâna Triban. It is Soumaoro's self-indulgence that allows Nâna to learn of his taboo. There is no real love between them. Soumaoro's weakness is not of the heart; it is merely physical passion, fueled by wine and the craftiness of the young woman. It brings to mind Sogolon's first advice to her son: "do not trust women with secrets, State or otherwise." The old king is not wise, which is particularly to be scorned in a culture so respectful of its elders, but he is also immoral in that he takes his nephew's wife, which is con-

sidered incest, and therefore unforgivable. In traditional African society, incest is viewed as an unacceptable act, and Soumaoro's inces-
tuous folly has alienated him from his own people and he has become
an outcast. He is portrayed as a morally wretched, fallen individual,
bringing about chaos and disorder, which is not only unbearable but
incomprehensible.

The character of Soumaoro is further complicated by the fact that
he is an artist, and his renown as a musician is as great as his fame
as a tyrant. According to Niane, tradition says that Soumaoro had
discovered the "Sossobala" or balafon (xylophone) in the forest of Tin-
iman on the river Niger, and it is the genie of the place that taught
him how to play it.[32] In the epic story, Soumaoro plays the balafon
and sings his own praises on it, acting as his own griot, and that is
why he feels the urge to keep Soundiata's griot because it is sweet to
hear one's praises. Balla Fassali, moreover, was a great musician, and
"the king of Sosso, flattered by the song and the melody that sustained it—was he not a man and therefore did he not share the weakness of men—said, 'I will no longer touch the balafon, from now on
you will be my griot, your duty will be to play the instrument after
each of my victories.' "[33]

Once again, Soumaoro breaks social conventions by taking someone else's griot and keeping him in captivity. However, he is not all
bad or worthless; there is at least one positive aspect to his personality, for he is a great musician. Moreover, he comes from a good family line and he is a great sorcerer, which implies great knowledge,
and is not necessarily negative. In the epic, however, his magical
powers are shown to be only a tool for his cruelty and evil deeds. He
has a special chamber in his castle in which he keeps terrifying human trophies and witchcraft paraphernalia attesting to the strength
and wickedness of his art. He dwells in an aura of evil and terror,
sure to capture the popular imagination and to act as the perfect foil
for the young and pure Soundiata.

Soumaoro exemplifies the flawed individual who, for no known reason, simply goes bad; we would call him mad. At first glance, tradition presents him as the embodiment of evil, but that is too simple
an answer. As Soundiata's antithesis, Soumaoro symbolizes more than
the moral principle of evil. He also represents chaos and social disorder in a highly structured and hierarchical society. Soundiata did
not come only to build an empire but to unite many lands and people
under one mind, one vision of the world. He is the Malinké's ideal

of social and political unity, harmony, and justice, and it is as a statesman that his name immortalized the Mali. This great political order sprang from the virtue of its founder and Soundiata's moral fiber took its source in Malinké metaphysics which stresses the control of the flesh or matter called *dya* for the benefit of the *ni* or spirit. Therefore, if Soumaoro is a barbarian and an evil man, it is not because he is an animist and a sorcerer but because he is a self-indulgent, asocial individual.

The bard sustains this idea very cleverly and Laye goes along with it, hinting that it is Soumaoro's humanity which is the cause of his evil. Was he not a man and therefore weak, asks the bard. It is not the powers that are bad, but the user. The struggle between Soumaoro and Soundiata is not the struggle between two sorcerers or two supernatural forces, as is often the case in legends; if it were, Soumaoro would win, his powers being so much greater than Soundiata's. In fact, except for Soumaoro's secret taboo, the supernatural, although omnipresent in the story, has very little impact on the development of the plot and the unfolding of the chain of events. Here, the clash between the two heroes has been somewhat demythologized, to emphasize their human side and perhaps for the sake of a certain psychological realism. It is no doubt the eternal struggle of good and evil, but in the concrete sense of virtue and vice in the Islamic and Malinké value system, and Laye reinforces the point by his symbolic use of colors—Soumaoro is all dressed in black and Soundiata all in white.

If the context of the work were clearly Islamic, it could be said that God was on Soundiata's side, but here, despite the religious overtones, it is rather destiny, the right, and the cleverness of women which are on the hero's side. He had been announced by prophecy as the savior and glory of the Manden, and he has made it come true by his virtue. It is through his kindness that he has obtained the help of Nâna Triban, who is only his half-sister and the daughter of Fatoumata, just as it is his righteousness and courage which endear him to his companions and secure for him the alliance of other leaders. By the same token, it is Soumaoro's vices and moral decay which allow him to conquer the Manden.

It has been argued that if the King of Sosso had not invaded the Manden and Dankaran Touman had not fled from his kingdom, Soundiata would not have been able to conquer the land without a fratricidal war, which would have been unacceptable to his righteousness. Everything in the story is set so as to allow the hero to express his goodness as a man, and the opposite is true for Soumaoro. The epic presents the struggle of two men locked into the inevitable duality of mankind, and good prevails over evil because the hero symbolizes the Malinké ideal. In the end, the legend of Soundiata is the pride of a culture and the dream of a nation.

Laye uses the character of Soumaoro to make a political statement. For him, the evil of the King of Sosso represents the contemporary tyrant, and his death is richly deserved. "Thus Soumaoro ended his life in that cave, he perished like all the tyrants of the world, abandoned and hated by everyone."[34] To describe the last moments of Soumaoro, the author once more draws from *Le Regard du roi* for some of his metaphors, and the king's final actions recall Clarence's anguish and awareness of his degradation. In Laye's version, Soumaoro regrets his evil deeds: "If he only could erase the life he had lived! But can we ever go back? If he could begin his reign again, he would be loyal toward the peoples of the Savannah and toward himself. He would adore God . . . he would recognize that Allah is supreme and one. . . ."[35] And the author goes on to praise the power and goodness of Allah, expressing his own faith but totally out of character with Soumaoro. Laye is preaching to the contemporary African politician and uses the ancient tyrant as the perfect example of what happens to leaders who use politics to satisfy their own selfish needs, to those who use Africa instead of serving it. This lesson in twentieth-century political ethics is fully in the spirit of the Master of the Word, whose mission is to guide and teach his people; however, it does not make good literature.

Soundiata

Okpewho points out that "the image of Sunjata as the champion and deliverer of his people, one destined by supernatural powers to save them and guarantee the right order of things, is established early in the story."[36] In Laye's version, the hero is also seen as symbolizing ancient African values, "these values [which] are, for the Malinké, an ethic consisting of generosity, loyalty, chivalry, [the] respect of the given word, the practice of Islam, the cora and the cola."[37] In Soundiata, then, Laye gives to the world and to his fellow countrymen an ideal image of man.

Soundiata may be an ideal, but he is human in that he has gone through the essential rites demanded of all Malinké, thus respecting the traditions established by the elders. He is loyal in his friendships, and the companions of the difficult years such as his half-brother Nan Boukari remain with him in his glory. His mind is as sound as his body, and great emphasis is placed on his intelligence, sagacity, ability to judge a situation, and self-control. The first king to receive him, for example, Mansa Konkon, paid by Fatoumata to dispose of him, challenges Soundiata to a game of Wori (a sort of chess game). The stake is Soundiata's life. Unperturbed, the young man accepts and wins despite his opponent's experience and great ability in the game. The king thinks he has been betrayed, but Soundiata points out to him that he would have to be a fool not to understand that the game was not just an innocent game, but a pretense masking a plot against his life. He reminds him that he had been at his court for several months and up to this day had never been asked for a game of Wori. Suddenly he is asked to play, and for no less than his life. Soundiata reinforces the sagacity of his remark by quoting an ancient proverb fitting the situation, thus demonstrating his knowledge and understanding of traditional wisdom and the fact that he cultivates the company of elders, who are the only source of ancient wisdom.

Laye adds a feminine twist to the incident (not in Niane) and tells that Soundiata had been warned of foul play by the daughter of the king who is in love with Nan Boukari. The author maximizes the role and influence of women in Soundiata's life, and his version seems to be the only one in which the hero has a lover. Her presence is very discreet and has no bearing on the action, but she is nevertheless mentioned twice and adds a sentimental and personal touch to an otherwise dutiful life, thus, perhaps, making the hero more appealing to a modern audience. Except for Fatoumata, the women characters are all positive and contradict traditional misogynism in a way that complies with contemporary trends and the narrator's own opinions.

Soundiata has the authority of a leader, the courage of a warrior, and the arrogance of a young man. In the battle scenes, his strength, valor, and abilities are amazing. The text is faithful to the epic genre in the descriptions of battles and of both armies, respect for the enemy, the boasting of the great warriors forming Soundiata's entourage, the numerous omens, the exaggerations; it reads like an African *Song of Roland*. It is during the exalted moments preceding the decisive battle of Kirina that Laye mentions the presence of his ancestor's totem, the black snake, which appears in the tent of Tabon Wana

Fran Camara as an omen of success. The tradition speaks of Fran Camara, and Niane mentions him in his version, but it can be assumed
that the presence of totems has very probably been added by the author, underlying once more the bond that Laye feels with the past
and its glory.

What of Soundiata's religious faith? In Laye's version the context
is Islamic for the reasons mentioned earlier; the name of Allah is in-
voked several times and Soumaoro's death is that of a believer who
has gone astray, although nowhere in the epic is there any reason to
believe that he was ever a Moslem. The Islamic context is artificial
and added on by the narrators, and most likely a recent addition to
the text. Babou Condé was a Moslem and an Arabic scholar, and it
could be that he wanted to "islamize" the text. But Laye's religious
beliefs appear fairly overtly, particularly at the end of the narrative
and especially during Soumaoro's death scene. However, Laye does
not go as far as to make Soundiata into a devout Moslem; the traditional text simply does not lend itself to such treatment, and Laye is
somewhat sympathetic to the traditional animist beliefs.

Soundiata's religion is ambiguous at best. He may dress like a
Moslem king but on the eve of battle the presence of the ancestral
totems reassures him, for they are a sign of victory. To insure success
at Kita, Soundiata had sacrificed many bulls to the genie which dwelt
in the waters of the mountain range surrounding the city. Later however, he sacrifices one hundred bulls to thank Allah for his victory on
Soumaoro. It is true that Islam tolerates certain animist beliefs under
the name of superstition, but Soundiata is definitely not an orthodox
Moslem, if he is one at all. What is certain is that he does not fight
Soumaoro under the banner of Islam. Soundiata is not a defender of
the faith; his war is not a *jihad,* and on this subject the text is quite
explicit. He fights the king of Sosso "to avenge his devastated country." He does mention that his fight has God's favor "because right
is on our side and God is on the side of the right,"[38] hardly the sort
of argument which promotes religious proselitism. Soundiata understands also that God and reason are not enough to win and does not
hesitate to use the spur of the white cock to insure victory. Ibrahima
Kake is surely right in thinking that Soundiata captures the popular
imagination because he remains faithful to his Malinké beliefs and
values, and thus stands for the spirit of the race.

What then is the image of Africa that can be drawn from the epic
of Soundiata? It is, of course, a glorious one, a moment of triumph

in a long history which is just beginning to become aware of itself. It is also the image of a civilization with its ethics and its mores, some of them still alive today, albeit threatened. For Laye, the past must feed the present and contemporary Africa is, in many respects, in need of a Soundiata or, in his more recent version, the Black Lion announced in *Dramouss*. He wanted to revive the spirit of the great Malinké hero, so that his countrymen would reflect on their past in order to build a better future.

As to the literary value of the work, it lacks the sobriety of Niane's version and it takes liberties with the facts, but Laye is an artist and not a historian. It has all the qualities and the faults of Laye's style: it is poetic and even flamboyant at times, but also sentimental and moralistic. The story is told with considerable skill in that it is action packed and fast moving. The numerous adventures of the main protagonists unfold rapidly and smoothly. The past, vividly re-created, attracts the attention and sustains the interest of the reader. There is a great insistence on the human element and daily living is described in detail. On the other hand, the battle scenes, which in most epics are too long and too numerous for the contemporary reader, are here handled with much restraint. Laye keeps the traditional form of the epic battle with its boasting, direct confrontation of the two enemy chiefs, the customary insults and taunting on both sides, the magnificence of the attire, and the exuberant display of courage and prowess of the warriors; all the epic elements are present but skillfully controlled and artistically condensed. Laye surely knows how to create an atmosphere and tell a good story. In that, he is the modern griot and therefore both the guardian of the past and the witness of his own time.

Chapter Six
Conclusion

Whatever else the twentieth century will be remembered for, one of its most memorable achievements will be the independence of the African continent. Camara Laye belonged to the last generation of Africans who, although raised as colonial subjects, became adults at the time of independence and could thus still reflect in their work the two different facets of African history. As successor to the Négritude movement, Laye's generation was the cornerstone of African letters, a group of writers who established beyond any doubt not only the existence of a written African literature, but the shaping of a written literary tradition as well.

Camara Laye stands as one of the most important West African writers to this day, for it is in his work that one finds the most complete and constant image of Africa, and an understanding of its spirit. His profound preoccupation with Africa is at the root of his sensibility and the source of his inspiration as an artist. The Nigerian writer Chinua Achebe has professed that the main function of African literature is to be useful to Africa, and this criterion, applicable to many other African writers, is indeed met in Laye's work. L'Enfant noir, a classic in its own time, is more than another variation on the theme of childhood; it is both a quest and an affirmation of one's own culture. It is a desire to comprehend the past in order to fit into the ever-changing present. As Proust explored the meandering of human time from the particular subjective vision of his protagonist, so Laye contemplated the protean image of Africa from his personal Guinean experiences. He too was in search of lost time, but in his case it was that of a people and of a continent. His last work, Le Maître de la parole, attests to his fascination with Africa's historical past, culture, and wisdom, a knowledge of which he considered essential to the successful shaping of the future.

Although L'Enfant noir is his best known and most widely read work, it is most likely Le Regard du roi which will immortalize Camara Laye. Few African novelists have as yet succeeded in creating a novel which transcends a particular African context to treat a theme common to all mankind, while still remaining faithful to a definite African sensibility. *Le Regard du roi* lifts the African novel from its provincial setting and sociological viewpoint and places it on a timeless philosophical level, thus entering it into world literature by the main entrance. No doubt, other African writers will achieve such a feat in the future, but Camara Laye will forever remain the one who opened that door.

Notes and References

Preface

1. The author's real name is actually Laye Camara, sometimes spelled Kamara. However, all his work is published under Camara Laye, which is the name he was given by the colonial school system.

2. According to the Guinean historian D. T. Niane, Mali and Malinké are the Fulani deformations of the words Manding and Mandinka. Manding or Mali refers to the land and Malinké to one of the ethnic groups living in that territory, and to their language and their culture.

3. See *The African Critic and his People as Producers of Civilization*, Proc. of the Yaoundé Colloquium, 16–20 April 1973 (Paris: Présence Africaine, 1977).

Chapter One

1. For this information I am indebted to Harold D. Nelson et al., *Area Handbook for Guinea*, 2d ed. (Washington, D.C.: Foreign Area Studies of the American University, 1976).

2. Jacqueline Sorel's interview of Camara Laye, *Cahiers de l'auditeur*, no. 1, Radio France Internationale, 1978.

3. The author was able to consult Laye's file at Editions Plon in Paris. It supplied a good deal of biographical information.

4. Négritude has been attacked by several English-speaking African writers, in particular the Nigerian playwright Wole Soyinka and the South African novelist and critic Ezekiel Mphalele. Although Soyinka thinks that Négritude should not be "underestimated or belittled" he sees it mostly as the problem of a small African elite in search of identity in the Metropolis of France. He insists that "Négritude proceeded along the route of over-simplification. Its re-entrenchment of black values was not preceded by any profound effort to enter into this African system of values." Wole Soyinka, *Myth, Literature and the African World* (Cambridge: Cambridge University Press, 1976), p. 127. On the other hand, Mphalele is annoyed by the fact that Négritude "romanticizes Africa as a symbol of innocence, purity and artless primitiveness." Quoted by Kofi Awoonor, *The Breast of the Earth* (New York: Anchor Press/Doubleday, 1975), p. 158.

5. Lilyan Kesteloot, *Anthologie Négro-Africaine* (Paris: Marabout Université, 1967), p. 82.

6. For this analysis I am indebted to Lilyan Kesteloot, *Négritude et Situation coloniale* (Yaoundé: Editions Clé, 1968), pp. 17–20.

7. Adèle King, *The Writings of Camara Laye* (London, 1980), p. 6.

8. Camara Laye, *Le Maître de la parole* (Paris, 1978), p. 14. "La civilisation, c'est peut-être une façon de faire et de vivre . . . Et les civilisations ont existé avant l'âge industriel, avant les progrès techniques qui en ont résulté, ces progrès que l'Afrique ne refuse pas, qu'elle attend au contraire impatiemment, mais qu'elle tient, qu'elle fera sagement de continuer de tenir, . . . pour complémentaires quant à la civilisation tout court."

9. Nelson et al., *Area Handbook for Guinea,* p. 35.

10. Malinké expression, literally, the suns of the Independences, expressing the glory of freedom. It is also the title of Ahmadou Kourouma's ironic novel (Paris: Seuil, 1970).

11. For this analysis I am indebted to Nelson et al., *Area Handbook for Guinea.* See also Ladipo Adamolekun, "L'agression du 22 novembre 1970," *Revue Française d'Etudes Politiques Africaines,* no. 114 (June 1975).

12. King, *Writings of Laye,* p. 10.

13. Gerald Moore, ed., *African Literature and the Universities* (Ibadan: Ibadan University Press and the Congress for Cultural Freedom, 1965), p. 10.

14. Adamolekun, "L'agression."

15. Alata's book was banned in France because it proved embarrassing for the Guinean government, with whom France had just renewed diplomatic ties. However, it is sold freely in Dakar. *La Danse et l'aveugle* was produced and directed by the Canadian Alain d'Aix and Morgane Laliberté. It won the prize of the FIFEF (Festival International du Film et des Échanges Francophones).

16. See "Prélude et fin d'un cauchemar," *Fraternité-Matin,* 17 December 1976: in this short story, Laye reworked Clarence's dream, the protagonist of *Le Regard du roi.* But in that version, Laye is the hero under the name of Ramaka and he is saved by a beautiful white woman who, although nameless, is evidently modeled on Mrs. Carducci.

17. In a private interview, Commandant Diallo, a Fulani from Guinea and a friend of Camara Laye, confirmed Laye's political involvement. Mr. Diallo is himself presently struggling against Touré's regime.

Chapter Two

1. *Colloque sur la littérature africaine d'expression française,* Faculté des lettres de Dakar, 26–29 March 1963. Quoted by Joyce A. Hutchinson in her edition of *L'Enfant noir* (Cambridge: Cambridge University Press, 1966), p. 7.

2. Eric Sellin, "Alienation in the Novels of Camara Laye," *Pan-African Journal* 4 (1971):455–72.

3. Charles Veillon is a Swiss patron of the arts who founded the International Prize of the French Novel. The winner receives 5000 Swiss francs.

4. Jean Blanzat, *Le Figaro Littéraire,* 6 March 1956. "Comment Camara

Laye ressent-il une métamorphose commencée depuis 1945 et qui va s'achever? Est-il partagé entre deux univers dissemblables? Comment juge-t-il celui où il a grandi, et dont il a appris nécessairement la singularité et les limites? Qu'en retient-il, et qu'en rejette-t-il? C'est sans doute la plus grande surprise qu'apporte ce livre. Pour Camara Laye, ces questions ne se posent pas. Il fait confiance aux Blancs, mais rien de ce qu'il apprend d'eux ne touche sa vie profonde. Il n'y a chez lui aucune inquiétude intellectuelle. Sa 'fidélité' est totale. Il ne se sent pas séparé des siens par aucune 'distance intérieure,' mais seulement par l'espace géographique. Il ne fait dans son esprit aucun tri pour garder ou rejeter: il garde tout, car si l'esprit a pu changer, l'esprit est resté le même.

Le témoignage de Camara Laye montre comment, dans un cas extrême, le coeur résout le problème: en l'ignorant!"

5. A. B. (Alexandre Biyidi, alias Mongo Beti), *"L'Enfant noir," Présence Africaine* 16 (1954):419–20.

6. Paul Edwards and Kenneth Ramchand, "An African Sentimentalist: Camara Laye's *The African Child," African Literature Today* 4 (1970):38.

7. Christophe Mfizi, "Laye Camara vu par un intellectuel Rwandais," *Bingo* 219 (April 1971):54, "J'ai choisi Laye Camara. D'abord parce que *L'Enfant noir* m'avait plu: il disait ce que j'aurais voulu dire après un séjour de deux ans en Belgique. *L'Enfant noir* c'était moi aussi."

8. Eustace Palmer, "Camara Laye: *The African Child,"* in his *An Introduction to the African Novel* (New York, 1972), p. 86.

9. King, *Writings of Laye,* p. 24.

10. Lilyan Kesteloot, *Anthologie négro-africaine* (Paris: Marabout Université, 1967), p. 193.

11. Léopold Sedar Senghor, "L'Esthétique négro-africaine," reprinted in *Liberté I: Négritude et Humanisme* (Paris: Seuil, 1964), pp. 209–10.

12. In an interview with *Fraternité-Matin,* 3 October 1972, Laye asserted that this repetitive rhythm attempts to capture the cadence of his native Malinké speech.

13. Camara Laye, "The Soul of Africa in Guinea," at the *Colloque sur la Littérature Africaine d'Expression Française,* Dakar, 1963. English translation published in G. D. Killam, ed., *African Writers on African Writing* (Evanston, Ill.: Northwestern University Press, 1973), p. 161.

14. Camara Laye, *L'Enfant noir,* ed. Joyce A. Hutchinson (Cambridge: Cambridge University Press, 1966), p. 29. All further page references refer to this edition. "[C]'est le génie de ton père . . . Bien que le merveilleux me fût familier, je demeurai muet tant mon étonnement était grand."

15. Ibid., p. 31: "—Ce serpent, dit-il, est le génie de notre race; comprends-tu? . . . Ce serpent, . . . est toujours présent; toujours il apparaît à l'un de nous. Dans notre génération, c'est à moi qu'il s'est présenté . . . Il s'est d'abord présenté sous forme de rêve."

16. Ibid., p. 32: "Je le dois au serpent, je le dois au génie de notre race."

17. Ibid., p. 33: ". . . Mais toujours est-il que si tu veux que le génie de notre race te visite un jour, si tu veux en hériter à ton tour, il faudra que tu adoptes ce même comportement; il faudra désormais que tu me fréquentes davantage."

18. J. E. Cirlot, *A Dictionary of Symbols,* trans. Jack Sage (New York: Philosophical Library, 1962), p. xiv.

19. Laye, *L'Enfant,* p. 35: "Pourtant j'aurais voulu, j'aurais tant voulu poser à mon tour ma main sur le serpent, comprendre, écouter à mon tour ce frémissement, mais j'ignorais comment le serpent eût accueilli ma main et je ne pensais pas qu'il eût maintenant rien à me confier, je craignais bien qu'il n'eût rien à me confier jamais. . . ."

20. Mircea Eliade, *Forgerons et Alchimistes* (Paris: Flammarion, 1977), p. 19: "Le forgeron est le principal agent de diffusion des mythologies, des rites et des mystères métallurgiques."

21. Ibid., p. 42: "L'or fut le premier métal découvert et utilisé par l'homme bien qu'il ne fût utilisé ni comme outil ni comme arme. Dans l'histoire de l'évolution technologique, pierre, bronze, fer, acier, l'or ne joua aucun rôle."

22. Mircea Eliade, *The Forge and the Crucible,* trans. Stephen Corrin (New York: Harper & Brothers, 1962), p. 144.

23. Laye, *L'Enfant,* p. 36: ". . . préludait sur sa cora, qui est notre harpe, et commençait à chanter les louanges de mon père."

24. Ibid., p. 42: "L'artisan qui travaille l'or doit se purifier au préalable, se laver complètement par conséquent et, bien entendu, s'abstenir, tout le temps de son travail, de rapports sexuels. Respectueux des rites comme il l'était, mon père ne pouvait manquer de se conformer à la règle. Or, je ne le voyais point se retirer dans sa case; je le voyais s'atteler à sa besogne sans préparation apparente. Dès lors il sautait aux yeux que, prévenu en rêve par son génie noir de la tâche qui l'attendait dans la journée, mon père s'y était préparé au saut du lit et était entré dans l'atelier en état de pureté. . . ."

25. Ibid., p. 39: "Le silence n'était interrompu que par le halètement des soufflets et le léger sifflement de l'or."

26. Ibid., p. 43: the English translation is by James Kirkup and Ernest Jones, *The Dark Child* (New York: Farrar, Strauss and Giroux, 1971, p. 43).

27. Eliade feels that, "There would appear to have existed . . . at several different cultural levels (which is a mark of very great antiquity), a close connection between the art of the smith, the occult sciences . . . and the art of song, dance and poetry." (Forgerons, Chap. 10, p. 99).

28. Gaston Bachelard, *L'Eau et les Rêves* (Paris: José Corti, 1971), pp. 156–57: "En résumé, l'amour filial est le premier principe actif de la projection des images, c'est la force projetante de l'imagination, force inépuisable qui s'empare de toutes les images pour les mettre dans la perspective humaine la plus sûre: la perspective maternelle."

29. Laye, *L'Enfant*, pp. 70–71: "Cela tenait, je crois bien, à la personne même de ma mère, qui imposait; cela tenait encore aux pouvoirs qu'elle détenait."

30. Ibid., p. 71: "Chez nous, il y a une infinité de choses qu'on n'explique pas, et ma mère vivait dans leur familiarité."

31. Ibid., p. 74: "Ce totem permettait à tous les Dâman de puiser impunément l'eau du fleuve Niger."

32. Ibid., p. 59: "En décembre, tout est en fleur et tout sent bon; tout est jeune; le printemps semble s'unir à l'été, et la campagne, longtemps gorgée d'eau, longtemps accablée de nuées maussades, partout prend sa revanche, éclate."

33. Edwards and Ramchand, "African Sentimentalist," p. 41.

34. Palmer, "Camara Laye," p. 92.

35. Laye, *L'Enfant*, p. 124: "A présent il y avait cette distance entre ma mère et moi: l'homme!"

Chapter Three

1. Interview, *La Presse du Cameroun*, 20 October 1966.

2. Charles R. Larson, *The Emergence of African Fiction* (Bloomington: Indiana University Press, 1972), p. 173.

3. Robert Pageard, "Du Témoignage à la vision prophétique: Dramouss," *Afrique-Document* 96 (January–February 1968):47: "Dramouss nous apporte l'un des premiers témoignages littéraires sur le conflit qui oppose l'esprit traditionnel africain au collectivisme autoritaire."

4. Chinua Achebe, "Africa and her Writers," in *In person: Achebe, Awonor, and Soyinka,* ed. Karen L. Morell (Seattle: University of Washington, 1975).

5. Jacqueline Leiner, "Interview avec Camara Laye," *Présence Francophone,* no. 10 (1975), p. 157: "Je n'y pensais plus. J'avais oublié mon obsession. C'est comme avec un docteur, j'étais guéri."

6. James Olney, *Tell me Africa* (Princeton: Princeton University Press, 1973), p. 149.

7. Camara Laye, *Dramouss* (Paris, 1966), p. 167. All further page references are to this edition.

8. The tale is widely known, and Pageard reports that, with a few variations, he heard the same tale in Ouagadougou. It also exists in written form in a collection called *Contes du Larhallé.*

9. Laye, *Dramouss,* p. 237.

10. Ibid., p. 227.

11. African hoe.

12. Camara Laye, "The Black Lion," in *African Literature and the Universities,* ed. Gerald Moore (Ibadan: Ibadan Press, 1965), p. 128.

13. King, *Writings of Laye.*

14. Roland Colin, quoted by King, *Writings of Laye*, p. 178.

15. Laye, *Dramouss*, p. 224.

16. Mircea Eliade, *Myth and Reality*, trans. Willard R. Trask (New York: Harper & Row, 1963), p. 54.

17. Laye, *Dramouss*, p. 225.

18. Cirlot, *Dictionary of Symbols*, p. 205.

19. Geoffrey Parrinder, *African Mythology* (London: Paul Hamlyn, 1967), p. 67.

Chapter Four

1. Camara Laye's original title was "Ciel d'Afrique," but Plon preferred *Le Regard du roi.*

2. Cheikh Hamidou Kane, *L'Aventure ambiguë* (Paris: Julliard, 1961).

3. Gabriel Okara, *The Voice* (London: André Deutsch, 1964).

4. Albert-Marie Schmidt, *Réforme*, 29 January 1955: ". . . Jamais nous n'avons rien lu de si dense, de si intime du Continent noir. . . ."

5. J. L. Curtis, "Laye Camara est un 'Kafka' revu par un Alain Fournier africain," *Art*, 11 January 1955. Quoted by J. J. Achiriga, *La Révolte des romanciers noirs de langue française* (Ottawa: Naaman, 1973), p. 60.

6. Wole Soyinka, "From a Common Black Cloth," *American Scholar* 32 (1963):387–88.

7. Camara Laye, "Nouvelles des lettres," *Dimanche-Matin*, 2 January 1955. "Le monde de Kafka n'est pas le mien. Si, comme Kafka et beaucoup d'autres, je crois 'qu'il n'y a rien d'autre qu'un monde spirituel,' c'est que ce monde-là est le mien depuis mon enfance, c'est que je n'ai jamais séparé le monde visible de l'Invisible . . . A la différence de Kafka et de ses personnages, jamais je ne me suis senti isolé, abandonné dans ce monde spirituel . . . J'y suis avec tous les hommes de ma race."

8. Camara Laye, *Fraternité-Matin*, 3 October 1972. "Le Regard du roi, roman écrit selon la technique de Kafka—non pas selon l'esprit, mais selon la technique de Kafka . . . Technique, qui à mon sens, est très proche de notre tempérament d'Africain."

9. Roland Barthes, *Le Degré zéro de l'écriture* (Paris: Le Seuil, 1972), p. 26. "Il suppose un monde construit, élaboré, détaché, réduit à des lignes significatives, et non un monde jeté, étalé, offert."

10. Seyyed Hossein Nasr, *Sufi Essays* (Albany: State University of New York Press, 1972), p. 27.

11. Janheinz Jahn, "Camara Laye: An Interpretation," *Black Orpheus* 6 (November 1959):36.

12. Wole Soyinka, *Myth, Literature and the African World* (Cambridge: Cambridge University Press, 1976), pp. 125–26.

13. Sunday O. Anozie, *Sociologie du roman africain* (Paris: Aubier-Montaigne, 1970), p. 181. "Ce que revendique Laye dans son oeuvre n'est

pas la réhabilitation de l'homme africain mais celle de l'homme universel
. . . Ce n'est donc pas tant ce qu'on a fait de l'homme qui compte, que ce
que l'homme fait de lui-même."

14. In an interview with Jacqueline Sorel, for the French radio, Laye explained that his father was a mystic and a deeply religious man who went
on religious retreats quite often. He was a man with a mystical conception
of God, and it is the paternal vision that the author tried to re-create in his
novel. Furthermore, Adèle King states in her book that Laye told her that
his father went on Sufi retreats.

15. David Cook, "The relevance of the King in Camara Laye's Le Regard
du roi," in *Perspectives on African Literature,* ed. C. Heywood (London: Heineman, 1971), p. 142.

16. Gaston Bachelard, *L'Eau et les rêves* (Paris: Corti, 1971), pp. 8–9.
". . . L'imagination matérielle de l'eau est un type particulier d'imagination
. . . et l'eau est aussi un type de destin, non plus seulement le vain destin
des images fuyantes, le vain destin d'un rêve qui ne s'achève pas, mais un
destin essentiel qui métamorphose sans cesse la substance de l'être . . .
L'être voué à l'eau est un être en vertige. Il meurt à chaque minute, sans
cesse quelque chose de sa substance s'écroule."

17. Camara Laye, *Le Regard du roi* (Paris, 1954), p. 28. All further
page references are to this edition. "—Tout me fuit, dit-il. Tout m'est obstacle. . . ."

18. Ibid. ". . . La barre qui défendait ces terres rouges et qu'il avait si
péniblement franchie . . . le flot vingt fois avait porté la barque vers le rivage et vingt fois l'avait rejetée vers la haute mer; puis la barque finalement
avait accosté."

19. Ben Obumselu, "The French and Moslem Backgrounds of the Radiance of the King," *Research in African Literatures* 2 (1980):20.

20. Laye, *Le Regard,* p. 11. ". . . Pris alors dans cette foule comme dans
une eau subitement figée ou dans un sable vaguement mouvant . . .";
p. 26: "—Est-ce que le roi est toujours entouré d'une mer aussi houleuse?"

21. Ibid., p. 89. ". . . Cette nappe de parfums, qui est comme la vraie
mer: la mer, déjà présente dans le vent et présente sur les lèvres, avant que
l'oeil ne la découvre . . . C'est cela d'abord, . . . mais ensuite, c'est une mer
sourdement travaillée, sourdement agitée; une mer avec ses courants et ses
fleuves secrets. . . ."

22. Bachelard, *L'Eau,* p. 206. "La mer donne des contes avant de donner
des rêves."

23. Laye, *Le Regard,* p. 128. ". . . L'eau communiquait au corps une
énergie très plaisante, une énergie dont on ne pouvait évidemment rien
faire, . . . une énergie gratuite, mais une énergie quand même."

24. Ibid., p. 11. "Il émanait de ces hommes étroitement agglomérés sous
le ciel d'Afrique une odeur de laine et d'huile, une odeur de troupeau, qui
plongeait l'être dans une espèce de sommeil."

25. Nasr, *Sufi Essays,* p. 33.

26. Laye, *Le Regard,* pp. 144–45. "Et qui aurait pu dire ce qui s'était passé? Clarence lui-même ne le savait pas. L'odeur de la forêt, sans doute; certainement cette odeur frôleuse qui est l'odeur même du Sud, aguicheuse et cruelle, lascive, inavouable. Mais Clarence la respirait avec dégoût, il y pensait avec dégoût . . . Il n'attendait pas la nuit: il la craignait. Le chien qui était en lui l'attendait peut-être; mais lui, il la craignait, il l'abominait."

27. Ibid., p. 151. "Je suis exactement comme eux. Et n'était-ce pas mieux ainsi? N'était-ce pas mieux que d'être Clarence? Et c'est pourquoi il suivait cette pente, qui était la pente des gens d'Aziana, qui n'était pas sa propre pente. Mais quelle était 'sa' pente?"

28. Ibid., p. 23. "Il est jeune et il est fragile, dit le mendiant, mais il est en même temps très vieux et il est robuste . . . S'il était moins chargé d'or, rien sans doute ne pourrait le retenir parmi nous."

29. Nasrallah S. Fatemi, Faramarz S. Fatemi, Fariborz S. Fatemi, *Sufism: Message of Brotherhood, Harmony and Hope* (South Brunswick, N.J.: A. S. Barnes and Co., 1976), p. 36.

30. Laye, *Le Regard,* p. 23. "Oui, il semblait qu'on pût aimer d'amour ce frêle adolescent, on le pouvait en dépit de la nuit de son teint . . . Mais pourquoi 'en dépit de la nuit de son teint'? . . . Qu'est-ce que le teint a de commun avec l'amour!"

31. Fatemi, *Sufism,* p. 59.

32. Laye, *Le Regard,* p. 24. "Le reflet d'une vie intérieure sans doute, mais de quelle vie? Peut-être de cette vie-là justement qui est au-delà de la mort . . . 'Est-ce cette vie que je suis venu chercher?' se demanda Clarence. Peut-être cette vie-là, oui."

33. Ibid., p. 120. "Le regard, rien que le regard, et tout serait dit, Tout! . . ."

34. Nasr, *Sufi Essays,* p. 57.

35. Laye, *Le Regard,* p. 16. "C'était ce mot 'faveur' qu'il ne pouvait digérer: il n'attendait aucune faveur! Il se proposerait au roi pour un travail ou l'autre, n'importe quel travail honorable, et il recevrait le juste prix de sa peine."

36. Nasr, *Sufi Essays,* p. 74.

37. Laye, *Le Regard,* p. 247. "—La chance, dit Clarence . . . Si j'avais le coeur à rire, je rirais. La chance . . . —Appelle la chose comme tu voudras, mais c'est le nom que je lui donne. Peut-être ne correspond-il à rien; et peut-être est-il le signe d'une chose réelle. Qu'en sais-tu? Ce que je sais, et cela je le sais à n'en pas douter, c'est que, si la chose existe, elle ne te sera pas donnée comme un don gratuit; tu n'en recevras pas plus que tu n'en extorqueras. Celui qui ne demande rien ne doit pas non plus s'étonner de s'en retourner les mains vides. Et enfin si personne n'est constamment favorisé, personne non plus n'est constamment frustré . . . La chance . . . Tu

vois à présent ce que je veux dire. Tu vois ce que j'appelle 'chance' et ce que d'autres appellent 'mérites.' —Le mendiant appelait cela 'faveur.'

....

— Donnez à la chose le nom qu'il vous plaira, dit Samba Baloum . . . laissez-moi l'appeler 'chance.' "

38. Henri Massé, *L'Islam* (Paris: Armand Colin, 1948), p. 106. "Tout homme a deux anges gardiens qui inscrivent ses actions bonnes et mauvaises. . . ."

39. Laye, *Le Regard,* pp. 186–87. "—Vous voulez dire que l'homme juste et l'homme injuste se valent?

— Je ne sais si c'est bien cela que j'ai voulu dire; je ne coupe pas les cheveux en quatre: je suis un forgeron. En fait, ce ne devrait pas être cela que j'ai voulu dire; mais, en fait encore, cela se ramène assez bien à cela.

— Mais cela ne devrait pas être! dit Clarence.

— Eh bien, dit Diallo, les hommes justes seraient beaucoup moins justes, je suppose, si leur justice flattait moins leur cruauté."

40. Ibid., p. 187. "Chaque jour et chaque heure, nous l'attendons. Mais nous nous lassons aussi de l'attendre. Et c'est quand nous sommes le plus las qu'il survient."

41. Ibid., p. 188. "Si bien que cette hache sera la somme de tout ce que j'ai appris, sera comme ma vie et l'effort de ma vie même. Mais que voulez-vous que le roi en fasse? . . . Il l'acceptera et ne l'admirera que pour me faire plaisir . . . Il aura toujours des haches infiniment plus belles et plus meurtrières que toutes celles que je pourrais forger . . . Pourtant je la forge . . . Peut-être ne puis-je faire autre chose, peut-être suis-je comme un arbre qui ne peut porter qu'une espèce de fruit. Et peut-être, en dépit de tant de défauts, peut-être parce que je suis comme cet arbre et que je manque de moyens, le roi malgré tout considérera-t-il ma bonne volonté."

42. Ibid., p. 189. "Il fut subitement l'enfant qui rougissait devant l'homme qu'il est devenu."

43. Ibid., p. 193. "Comme si la fraîcheur de l'eau lui eût fait signe."

44. Ibid. "Jaune et lourd, entre des rives boueuses."

45. Ibid., p. 194. "L'odeur s'était beaucoup épaissie; elle tombait des cimes et elle montait du sol; et il y avait quelque part un lieu de rencontre, un lieu mouvant qui, par intervalle, refluait vers Clarence et le submergeait."

46. Bachelard, *L'Eau,* p. 49. "L'être qui sort de l'eau est un reflet qui peu à peu se matérialise: il est une image avant d'être un être, il est un désir avant d'être une image."

47. Laye, *Le Regard,* p. 194. "Au milieu du fleuve, à proximité d'une île qui était au milieu du fleuve, une vague forme de femme émergeait. Une forme vague; car si les seins étaient visiblement des seins de femme, la tête était bien plus une tête de poisson qu'une tête de femme."

48. M. de Lestrange, "Génies de l'eau et de la brousse en Guinée

française," *Etudes guinéennes* 4 (1950):11. "A Siguiri, à Kankan ou à Kurusa chacun sait pourquoi le lamentin qui vit dans les eaux du Niger, a des seins de femme. Une femme était en train de se baigner dans le fleuve. Elle était nue. Son gendre est arrivé et elle n'a eu le temps que de se couvrir d'un léfa (couvercle de vannerie) et de se jeter à l'eau. De honte elle n'a jamais osé revenir sur terre. La forme circulaire de sa queue rappelle celle du léfa. Les Somoro, pêcheurs du Niger, ne tuent pas le lamentin qui descend d'un être humain."

49. Laye, *Le Regard,* p. 195. "La forme, à présent, progressait en ondulant parmi les herbes et paraissait brouter. Chaque fois qu'elle se renversait, ses seins se découvraient, opulents et blanchâtres . . . on pensait à des femmes, on ne pouvait penser qu'à des femmes."

50. Bachelard, *L'Eau,* p. 189. "L'impureté, au regard de l'inconscient, est toujours multiple."

51. Laye, *Le Regard,* p. 197. "L'eau, en même temps qu'elle s'était épaissie, avait perdu sa fâcheuse coloration jaune; elle était argentée et parsemée d'ombres d'un beau bleu métallique."

52. Bachelard, *L'Eau,* p. 152. "Les rêves qui ont vécu dans une âme continuent de vivre dans ses oeuvres."

53. Laye, *Le Regard,* p. 199. "Clarence vit le moment où il n'allait pas seulement les frôler, mais les heurter; heurter en plein leurs seins blanchâtres."

54. Ibid., p. 200. "Le ciel était plein d'étoiles, et rien n'interceptait la vue, ni voûte de feuillages, ni voûte d'aucune sorte. . . ."

55. For the information on Malinké metaphysics I am indebted to Moussa Oumar Sy, "L'Esprit et la matière dans la métaphysique manding," Colloque sur la civilisation mandingue. Londres du 1er au 5 Juillet, 1972, and to Sory Camara, "Gens de la parole: essai sur la condition et le rôle des griots dans la société malinké," Diss. Université de Bordeaux 1969, pp. 219–20.

56. Laye, *Le Regard,* p. 210. "Mais c'était la franchise de l'abjection, seulement; c'était pur cynisme."

57. Ibid., p. 211. "—Elle ne dit jamais tout, dit Nagoa. Elle découvre les choses et elle les fait voir. Mais on ne les découvre et on ne les voit à son tour que si on prend la peine de les bien regarder."

58. Ibid., p. 223. "A présent tu sais . . . Va maintenant . . . Laisse-moi . . . —Sache qu'il n'y a pas de femme si vieille qu'on ne puisse la maltraiter."

59. Ibid., p. 219. "Il ne pouvait jamais voir aucun visage de femme, sauf dans l'encadrement d'une fenêtre; mais Dioki, il la voyait parfaitement. Les autres, quand il les rencontrait, il ne voyait que leurs seins ou leur croupe; ses yeux ne pouvaient se détacher de leurs seins ou de leur croupe; mais, Dioki, il la voyait toute. Elle avait des seins si flétris que le regard ne par-

venait pas à s'y attarder; quant à sa croupe, elle avait fondu; on eût juré qu'elle n'avait plus de croupe."

60. Cirlot, *Dictionary of Symbols,* p. 95.

61. Nasr, *Sufi Essays,* p. 43.

62. Laye, *Le Regard,* pp. 238–39. "—Un coq! voilà tout ce que tu es, dit-il. C'est comme coq que le mendiant t'a vendu au naba, et c'est en coq que tu t'es comporté . . . Un coq n'est pas digne de paraître devant le roi, dit le maître des cérémonies . . . Impur comme tu l'es, tu n'es bon qu'à être enfermé dans le sérail!"

63. Ibid., p. 248. "Des nabas, les hommes en fabriquent tous les jours de nouveaux. Le roi est là, et le naba n'est plus rien, le naba est de la crotte de chien."

64. Laye, *L'Enfant,* p. 167. ". . . Je pense que Check nous a précédé sur le chemin de Dieu . . . qui est certainement moins effrayant que l'autre . . . le chemin de la vie . . . qui n'est jamais que le chemin momentané de notre exil. . . ."

65. Laye, *Le Regard,* p. 243. "Clarence sentit le sang de la honte se répandre sur ses joues . . . Mais était-ce vraiment à lui de rougir? Avait-il tant de pudeur? . . . Il ne rougissait pas! il était l'acteur même de ce mime et il n'avait pas honte . . . Mais pourquoi était-ce ce mime qu'on avait choisi de représenter devant le roi? N'était-ce pas faire injure au roi, insulter sa pureté? Ou la simple présence du roi retranchait-elle son ignominie au mime? . . . Peut-être suffisait-il que le roi fût présent pour que tout devînt pur. . . ."

66. Ibid., p. 246. "Tu es aussi digne de te présenter que n'importe quel autre. Si tous ceux qui se présentent devant le roi devaient être dignes de lui, le roi vivrait dans un désert."

67. Ibid., p. 245. "—Il est toujours trop tard, dit Diallo. A peine sommes-nous nés, qu'il est déjà trop tard. Mais le roi ne l'ignore pas, et c'est pourquoi aussi il est toujours temps."

68. Nasr, *Sufi Essays,* p. 48.

69. Ibid., p. 74.

70. Laye, *Le Regard,* p. 249. "Quelque chose qui ressemble à la vie, pensait-il vaguement. Quelque chose qui peut-être est la vie même: une pure folie et une sarabande de fols!"

71. Ibid. "—Est-ce ainsi quand on meurt? dit-il à voix basse. Sans doute était-ce ainsi; on reposait dans une lumière diffuse, une lumière douce et drue . . . Mais d'où venait cette lumière? . . . Alors il vit le roi."

72. Ibid., p. 252. "Quand il fut parvenu devant le roi, quand il fut dans le grand rayonnement du roi, et tout meurtri encore par le trait de feu, mais tout vivant et seulement vivant de ce feu, Clarence tomba à genoux, car il lui semblait qu'il était enfin au bout de sa course et au terme de toute course.

Mais sans doute ne s'était-il pas assez approché encore, sans doute était-il trop timide encore, car le roi lui ouvrit les bras. Et dans le temps qu'il lui ouvrait les bras, son manteau s'entrouvrit, son mince torse d'adolescent se découvrit. Sur ce torse, dans la nuit de ce torse, il y avait—au centre, mais pas tout à fait au centre, un peu sur la droite—un léger battement qui faisait frémir la peau. C'était ce battement qui appelait, ce léger battement! C'était ce feu qui brûlait et cette lumière qui rayonnait. C'était cet amour qui dévorait.

—Ne savais-tu pas que je t'attendais? dit le roi.

Et Clarence posa doucement les lèvres sur le léger, sur l'immense battement. Alors le roi referma lentement les bras, et son grand manteau enveloppa Clarence pour toujours."

73. Henri Corbin, *Histoire de la philosophie islamique* (Paris: Gallimard, 1964), p. 281. "Lorsque l'amour existe réellement, l'amant devient la nourriture de l'Aimé; ce n'est pas l'Aimé qui est la nourriture de l'amant, car l'Aimé ne peut être contenu dans la capacité de l'amant [. . .] Le papillon qui est devenu l'amant de la flamme, a pour nourriture, tant qu'il est encore à distance, la lumière de cette aurore. C'est le signe avant-coureur de l'illumination matutinale qui l'appelle et qui l'accueille. Mais il lui faut continuer de voler jusqu'à ce qu'il la rejoigne. Lorsqu'il y est arrivé, ce n'est plus à lui de progresser vers la flamme, c'est la flamme qui progresse en lui. Ce n'est pas la flamme qui lui est une nourriture, c'est lui qui est la nourriture de la flamme. Un instant fugitif il devient son propre Aimé (puisqu'il est la flamme). Et sa perfection, c'est cela."

74. King, *Writings of Laye,* p. 44.

Chapter Five

1. In an interview with *Fraternité-Matin,* 5 April 1976.

2. Djibril Tamsir Niane, *Soundjata ou l'épopée mandingue* (Paris: Présence Africaine, 1960).

3. Massa Makan Diabaté, *Kala jata* (Bamako: Ed. Populaires, 1970).

4. Massa Makan Diabaté, *L'Aigle et l'épervier ou la geste de Sunjata, poème populaire* (Paris: Pierre-Jean Oswald, 1975).

5. Gordon Innes, *Sunjata, Three Mandinka Versions* (London: School of Oriental and African Studies, University of London, 1974), p. 30. Innes disagrees with Niane as to the existence of Griot training centers.

6. The name of the Malinké hero is spelled differently following the versions. These variations are due in part to the symbolic interpretations which enter into the formation of the hero's name, and the fact that the spelling of Malinké has not been codified. Sometimes it is also spelled phonetically "Sondjata" which is how it sounds in Malinké.

7. Ibrahima Baba Kake, "La civilisation de la boucle du Niger du XIe au XVIe siècle," *Présence Africaine* 89 (1974):78. "On peut distinguer quatre

grandes périodes dans l'histoire du Mali: 1) Des origines au XIIIe siècle; 2) L'empire de Soundiata et de ses successeurs; 3) L'âge d'or de l'empire, le XIVe siècle; 4) L'effritement: XVe et XVIe siècles."

8. Djibril Tamsir Niane, "Histoire et tradition historique du Manding," *Présence Africaine* 89 (1974):60. "Le corpus a été le premier effort pour procurer à l'aristocratie malinké une image d'elle et du monde destinée à la calmer. Il y a ici comme un refus du temps, un classicisme décadent; la contemplation d'un passé devenu idéal et idéalisé."

9. Ibid., p. 67.

"— La genèse du Manding, des origines à Soundjata, les Keïta sont censés descendre de Bilal, le premier Noir muezzin de l'Islam;

— La généalogie de tous les compagnons de Soundjata, artificiellement rattachés à des personnages bibliques ou à des saints de l'Islam;

— La geste proprement dite de Soundjata ou Soundjata-Fassa qui a donné son nom au Corpus: il s'agit des exploits guerriers de Soundjata et de ses principaux généraux;

— Plusieurs chants épiques qui constituent la grande musique mandingue;

— La constitution politique et sociale de l'empire;

— La liste des seize clans malinké et des cinq clans maraboutiques du Mali;

— Les us et coutumes du temps de Soundjata."

10. For this presentation I am indebted to Sory Camara, "Gens de la parole: essai sur la condition et le rôle des griots dans la société malinké," Diss. Université de Bordeaux 1969.

11. Camara Laye, *Le Maître de la parole* (Paris, 1978). p. 60. All further page references are to this edition and all English translations my own. "La parole était un art femelle exclusivement réservé aux griots et aux femmes. . . ."

12. For this information, I am indebted to Niane's article (see note 8).

13. Laye, *Le Maître,* p. 31. "Il était . . . le détenteur de la chaire de l'histoire de toutes les régions de Kouroussa, ces régions peuplées de près de cent mille âmes."

14. Ibid., pp. 85–86. "Par Allah, la fille qui viendra, encadrée par deux jeunes gens, dit-il, il faudra l'épouser! Elle mettra au monde un fils qui s'imposera à tous les pays de la savane . . . Il rendra le nom du Mandén immortel à jamais."

15. Ibid., p. 163. "A partir d'aujourd'hui, c'est devant ta case que les femmes de Niani—Fatoumata comprise!—viendront s'approvisionner."

16. Knowledge is always esoteric in ancient Africa. Niane reports that the griots of Keyla, a village on the river Niger, are known to hold the secrets of the old Manding. This is contested by other griots who, in turn, claim to know a more genuine tradition. However, the secret of Soundiata's death is still intact.

17. C. M. Bowra, *Heroic Poetry* (London: Macmillan, 1952).

18. Ruth Finnegan, *Oral Literature in Africa* (Oxford: Clarendon Press, 1970), pp. 108–10. Surprisingly, this excellent book devotes only a three-page note to the epic, claiming that it does not really exist in Africa since the African heroic narratives are in prose and not in verse.

19. Isodore Okpewho, *The Epic in Africa* (New York: Columbia University Press, 1979).

20. Lilyan Kesteloot, "Les épopées de l'ouest africain," *Présence Africaine* 58 (1966):205–6. ". . . L'épopée africaine possède en effet toutes les caractéristiques du genre épique traditionnel: non seulement le fondement historique indispensable, avec les déviations dus à l'embellissement des faits, le désir de plaire au prince, l'imagination populaire et le recul du temps, mais encore l'intervention du merveilleux, depuis le grossissement des exploits et de la force des héros, jusqu'à la coopération personnelle des dieux, les sorciers et les animaux-totems remplacent ici les saints et les anges."

21. Okpewho, *Epic in Africa,* p. 154.

22. King, *Writings of Laye,* pp. 90, 92.

23. Okpewho, *Epic in Africa,* p. 232.

24. Laye, *Le Maître,* p. 105. "Ce fut bientôt un fleuve de mains levées . . . les enfants . . . se mêlaient à la houle du cortège."

25. Ibid., p. 78. "Son être profond, il s'en rendait compte, était la somme de deux 'moi' intimes. Le premier, tout à fait conforme à son sens de la vie, façonné par son existence d'esclave corvéable, ayant impérieusement besoin de s'appuyer sur sa foi en l'Etre Suprême pour subsister, combattait le second, personnage bourré de complexes et vaguement raciste, espérant être l'égal des Arabes en s'enduisant le corps de cendre pour se blanchir la peau."

26. Ibid., p. 39. "Qu'était (une femme) à cette époque lointaine sinon un instrument dont le devoir était de mettre des enfants au monde, de les élever, et qui n'avait pas le même droit que l'homme dans le partage de l'héritage? Nous ne l'expliquons pas clairement, encore que depuis, les Malinké de Sangaran se soient ressaisis, et aient réhabilité la femme, en la hissant au même niveau que l'homme."

27. Ibid., p. 170. "—Non, nous le lui dirons ensemble. Nous ne serons pas trop de deux, tu peux m'en croire!"

28. Laye, *L'Enfant,* p. 172.

29. Laye, *Le Maître,* pp. 172–73. "Aime ta femme, mais ne lui confie jamais de secrets d'État! . . . Un roi n'a pas d'ami! . . . Le fils d'un autre n'est pas ton fils! Le pays d'un autre n'est pas ton pays! . . . Un royaume ne peut fonctionner sans le concours des vieux!"

30. Ibid., p. 177. ". . . La terre natale, en dépit de l'hospitalité qu'on peut trouver en d'autres pays—le pays hôte ignore le rang social!—la terre natale sera toujours plus qu'une simple terre: c'est toute la Terre!"

31. Robert Pageard, "Soundiata Keita et la tradition orale," *Présence Africaine* 36 (1961):65.

32. According to Niane, *Histoire et Tradition,* Soumaoro was the first "balafoniste" of the Manden and he supposedly invented many other instruments. In the village of Niagassola, one can see the famous balafon of Soumaoro, which is very large and played only on specific days. The guardian of the instrument is always an old man, so as to insure that only traditional music is played on it. The tradition of Niagassola is rich in details of the life of the king, as well as the religious practices and magic of the old Manden (see note 8, pp. 63–64).

33. Laye, *Le Maître,* p. 206. "Le souverain de Sosso, flatté par ce chant et par la mélodie qui l'accompagnait—n'était-il pas un homme et ne partageait-il pas la faiblesse des hommes?—déclara. . .—Je ne toucherai plus à ce balafon, tu seras désormais mon griot, ton devoir sera de jouer cet instrument après chacune de mes victoires."

34. Ibid., p. 245. "Ainsi, Soumaoro finit dans cette grotte, comme périssent tous les tyrans de la terre, abandonné et haï de tout le monde. . . ."

35. Ibid., p. 244. "S'il avait pu abolir sa vie! . . . Mais revient-on sur ses pas? S'il pouvait recommencer son règne, il serait loyal avec les peuples de la savane et avec lui-même. Il adorerait Dieu . . . il reconnaîtrait que Allah est Unique et Suprême. . . ."

36. Okpewho, *Epic in Africa,* p. 127.

37. Laye, *Le Maître,* p. 14. "Ces valeurs, sont chez les Malinké une éthique comportant la générosité, la loyauté, la chevalerie, le respect de la parole donnée, la pratique de l'Islam, la cora et la cola." In a note, Laye explains that the cora is an African harp of twenty-one strings and the cola is a fruit which is usually given as a social gesture much like flowers in Europe.

38. Ibid., p. 217. ". . . Parce que la raison est de notre côté et Dieu est du côté de la raison."

Selected Bibliography

PRIMARY SOURCES

1. Novels

Dramouss. Paris: Plon, 1966. Reprint. Paris: Presses Pocket, 1976.

A Dream of Africa. Translated by James Kirkup. London: Collins, 1968. Reprint. New York: Collier Books, 1971.

L'Enfant noir. Paris: Plon, 1953. Reprint. Paris: Presses Pocket, 1976.

The Dark Child. Translated by James Kirkup. London: Collins, 1955. Reprints. New York: Noonday Press, 1954; New York: Farrar, Straus and Giroux, 1969.

Le Maître de la parole. Paris: Plon, 1978.

The Guardian of the Word. Translated by James Kirkup. London: Collins, 1980.

Le Regard du roi. Paris: Plon, 1954. Reprint. Paris: Presses de la Cité, 1975.

The Radiance of the King. Translated by James Kirkup. London: Collins, 1956. Reprint. New York: Collier Books, 1965 and 1971.

2. Short Stories

"Les Yeux de la statue." *Présence Africaine* 13 (1957):102–10.

"The Eyes of the Statue." Translated by Una Maclean. *Black Orpheus* 5 (1959):10–27. Reprinted in *More Modern African Stories.* Edited by Charles R. Larson. London: Fontana-Collins, 1975.

"Prélude et fin d'un cauchemar." *Fraternité-Matin,* 17 December 1976.

3. Essays

"The Black Man and Art." *African Arts* 4 (1970):58–59.

"Et Demain?" *Présence Africaine* 14–15 (1957):290–95.

"Premier contact avec Paris." *Bingo* 14 (1954):21–22.

4. Published and Unpublished Lectures

"L'Afrique et l'appel des profondeurs." Fourah Bay Conference, 1963. Edited and translated by Gerald Moore as "The Black Lion." *Black Orpheus* 14 (1964):21–24.

"L'Ame de l'Afrique dans sa partie guinéenne." Colloque sur la Littérature Africaine d'Expression Française, Dakar. 1963. Reprinted in English in *African Literature and the Universities.* Edited by Gerald Moore. Ibadan:

Ibadan University Press, 1965. Also in *African Writers on African Writing*. Edited by G. D. Killam. Evanston: Northwestern University Press, 1973.

"Le Rêve dans la société traditionnelle malinké." Paper read at Conference on Manding Studies, 1972, at School of Oriental and African Studies, University of London.

SECONDARY SOURCES

1. Book

King, Adèle. *The Writings of Camara Laye.* London: Heinemann, 1980. The only book on Laye so far, and a very good introduction to the author and his work. Excellent bibliography.

2. Articles and Chapters in Books

Achiriga, J. J. *"L'Enfant noir* and *Le Regard du roi."* In: *La Révolte des romanciers noirs de langue française.* Ottawa: Naaman, 1973, pp. 32–65. Interesting interpretation of Laye's novels and good analysis of the author's controversial position in the African literary milieu.

Anozie, Sunday O. "La Grâce apocalyptique chez Camara Laye ou le mysticisme de l'amour." In: *Sociologie du roman africain.* Paris: Aubier-Montaigne, 1970, pp. 170–87. Studies the themes and structures of Laye's *Le Regard du roi.* Disagrees with Jahn's interpretation.

Edwards, Paul and Ramchand, Kenneth. "An African Sentimentalist: Camara Laye's *The African Child." African Literature Today* 4 (1970):37–53. The authors feel that Laye gives a sentimental and sometimes trivial view of traditional Africa. They consider the last four chapters to be poorly crafted.

Ita, J. M. "Laye's *Radiance of the King* and Kafka's *Castle." Odù* 4 (1970):18–45. A defense of Laye's novel, which had been criticized by Soyinka as being a derivative of Kafka's *Castle.* The author demonstrates that the novel is not a derivative of Kafka but an African version of it.

Jahn, J. *"Camara Laye: An Interpretation." Black Orpheus* 6 (1959):35–38. Interesting and controversial interpretation based on African philosophy. Discusses *The Radiance of the King* in light of *The Dark Child* because he sees a philosophical continuity in both novels. Disagrees with Ramsaran's analysis of Laye's second novel.

Larson, Charles R. "Assimilated Negritude: Camara Laye's *Le Regard du roi."* In: *The Emergence of African Fiction.* Bloomington: Indiana University Press, 1972, pp. 167–226. Finds the novel an affirmation of Négritude. This one-sided view results in an oversimplification of the book's symbolism. However, contains many valuable ideas.

Moore, Gerald. "Camara Laye: Nostalgia and Idealism." In: *Seven African Writers*. London: Oxford University Press, 1962, pp. 25–38. Examines simultaneously *The Dark Child* and *The Radiance of the King*. Solid and safe study of Laye's work.

Obumselu, Ben. "The French and Moslem Backgrounds of *The Radiance of the King*." *Research in African Literatures* 2, no. 1 (Spring 1980):1–25. Excellent article on the influences of Sufi mysticism on the symbolism of Laye's novel. Supersedes Ramsaran's article on the subject.

Pageard, Robert. "Du Témoignage à la vision prophétique: *Dramouss*." *Afrique-Document* 96 (January–February 1968):45–50. Although flawed, the only valid article on *Dramouss* presently available.

Palmer, Eustace. "Camara Laye: *The African Child*." In: *An Introduction to the African Novel*. New York: Africana Publishing Co., 1972, pp. 85–95. Good analysis. The author takes into consideration the best-known criticism of the book.

Scheub, Harold. "Symbolism in Camara Laye's *Le Regard du roi*." *Ba Shiru* 1 (Spring 1970):24–36. Intelligent and tightly argued essay.

Index